Fractions and Area

Different Shapes, Equal Pieces

Grade 4

Also appropriate for Grades 5 and 6

Cornelia Tierney
Mark Ogonowski
Andee Rubin
Susan Jo Russell

Contributing Author
Rebecca B. Corwin

Developed at TERC, Cambridge, Massachusetts

Dale Seymour Publications®
Menlo Park, California

The *Investigations* curriculum was developed at TERC (formerly
Technical Education Research Centers) in collaboration with Kent State
University and the State University of New York at Buffalo. The work was
supported in part by National Science Foundation Grant No. ESI-9050210.
TERC is a nonprofit company working to improve mathematics and science
education. TERC is located at 2067 Massachusetts Avenue, Cambridge,
MA 02140.

This project was supported, in part,
by the
National Science Foundation
Opinions expressed are those of the authors
and not necessarily those of the Foundation

Managing Editor: Catherine Anderson

Series Editor: Beverly Cory

Revision Team: Laura Marshall Alavosus, Ellen Harding, Patty Green Holubar,
Suzanne Knott, Beverly Hersh Lozoff

ESL Consultant: Nancy Sokol Green

Production/Manufacturing Director: Janet Yearian

Production/Manufacturing Coordinator: Joe Conte

Design Manager: Jeff Kelly

Design: Don Taka

Illustrations: Hollis Burkhart, Barbara Epstein-Eagle

Cover: Bay Graphics

Composition: Archetype Book Composition

This book is published by Dale Seymour Publications®, an imprint of
Addison Wesley Longman, Inc.

Dale Seymour Publications
2725 Sand Hill Road
Menlo Park, CA 94025
Customer Service: 800-872-1100

Order number DS43894
ISBN 1-57232-747-2
1 2 3 4 5 6 7 8 9 10-ML-01 00 99 98 97

 Printed on Recycled Paper

T E R C

Principal Investigator   Susan Jo Russell

Co-Principal Investigator   Cornelia C. Tierney

Director of Research and Evaluation   Jan Mokros

Curriculum Development
Joan Akers
Michael T. Battista
Mary Berle-Carman
Douglas H. Clements
Karen Economopoulos
Ricardo Nemirovsky
Andee Rubin
Susan Jo Russell
Cornelia C. Tierney
Amy Shulman Weinberg

Evaluation and Assessment
Mary Berle-Carman
Abouali Farmanfarmaian
Jan Mokros
Mark Ogonowski
Amy Shulman Weinberg
Tracey Wright
Lisa Yaffee

Teacher Support
Rebecca B. Corwin
Karen Economopoulos
Tracey Wright
Lisa Yaffee

Technology Development
Michael T. Battista
Douglas H. Clements
Julie Sarama Meredith
Andee Rubin

Video Production
David A. Smith

Administration and Production
Amy Catlin
Amy Taber

**Cooperating Classrooms
for This Unit**
Angela Philactos
Michele de Silva
Meg Watson
Boston Public Schools
Boston, MA

Kathleen D. O'Connell
Jane Healy
Arlington Public Schools
Arlington, MA

Consultants and Advisors
Elizabeth Badger
Deborah Lowenberg Ball
Marilyn Burns
Ann Grady
Joanne M. Gurry
James J. Kaput
Steven Leinwand
Mary M. Lindquist
David S. Moore
John Olive
Leslie P. Steffe
Peter Sullivan
Grayson Wheatley
Virginia Woolley
Anne Zarinnia

Graduate Assistants
Kent State University
Joanne Caniglia
Pam DeLong
Carol King

State University of New York at Buffalo
Rosa Gonzalez
Sue McMillen
Julie Sarama Meredith
Sudha Swaminathan

Revisions and Home Materials
Cathy Miles Grant
Marlene Kliman
Margaret McGaffigan
Megan Murray
Kim O'Neil
Andee Rubin
Susan Jo Russell
Lisa Seyferth
Myriam Steinback
Judy Storeygard
Anna Suarez
Cornelia Tierney
Carol Walker
Tracey Wright

CONTENTS

WHERE TO START

The first-time user of *Different Shapes, Equal Pieces* should read the following:

When you next teach this same unit, you can begin to read more of the background. Each time you present the unit, you will learn more about how your students understand the mathematical ideas.

Investigations in Number, Data, and Space® is a K–5 mathematics curriculum with four major goals:

- to offer students meaningful mathematical problems
- to emphasize depth in mathematical thinking rather than superficial exposure to a series of fragmented topics
- to communicate mathematics content and pedagogy to teachers
- to substantially expand the pool of mathematically literate students

The *Investigations* curriculum embodies a new approach based on years of research about how children learn mathematics. Each grade level consists of a set of separate units, each offering 2–8 weeks of work. These units of study are presented through investigations that involve students in the exploration of major mathematical ideas.

Approaching the mathematics content through investigations helps students develop flexibility and confidence in approaching problems, fluency in using mathematical skills and tools to solve problems, and proficiency in evaluating their solutions. Students also build a repertoire of ways to communicate about their mathematical thinking, while their enjoyment and appreciation of mathematics grows.

The investigations are carefully designed to invite all students into mathematics—girls and boys, members of diverse cultural, ethnic, and language groups, and students with different strengths and interests. Problem contexts often call on students to share experiences from their family, culture, or community. The curriculum eliminates barriers—such as work in isolation from peers, or emphasis on speed and memorization—that exclude some students from participating successfully in mathematics. The following aspects of the curriculum ensure that all students are included in significant mathematics learning:

- Students spend time exploring problems in depth.
- They find more than one solution to many of the problems they work on.

- They invent their own strategies and approaches, rather than relying on memorized procedures.
- They choose from a variety of concrete materials and appropriate technology, including calculators, as a natural part of their everyday mathematical work.
- They express their mathematical thinking through drawing, writing, and talking.
- They work in a variety of groupings—as a whole class, individually, in pairs, and in small groups.
- They move around the classroom as they explore the mathematics in their environment and talk with their peers.

While reading and other language activities are typically given a great deal of time and emphasis in elementary classrooms, mathematics often does not get the time it needs. If students are to experience mathematics in depth, they must have enough time to become engaged in real mathematical problems. We believe that a minimum of five hours of mathematics classroom time a week—about an hour a day—is critical at the elementary level. The plan and pacing of the *Investigations* curriculum is based on that belief.

We explain more about the pedagogy and principles that underlie these investigations in Teacher Notes throughout the units. For correlations of the curriculum to the NCTM Standards and further help in using this research-based program for teaching mathematics, see the following books:

- *Implementing the* Investigations in Number, Data, and Space® *Curriculum*
- *Beyond Arithmetic: Changing Mathematics in the Elementary Classroom* by Jan Mokros, Susan Jo Russell, and Karen Economopoulos

This book is one of the curriculum units for *Investigations in Number, Data, and Space.* In addition to providing part of a complete mathematics curriculum for your students, this unit offers information to support your own professional development. You, the teacher, are the person who will make this curriculum come alive in the classroom; the book for each unit is your main support system.

Although the curriculum does not include student textbooks, reproducible sheets for student work are provided in the unit and are also available as Student Activity Booklets. Students work actively with objects and experiences in their own environment and with a variety of manipulative materials and technology, rather than with a book of instruction and problems. We strongly recommend use of the overhead projector as a way to present problems, to focus group discussion, and to help students share ideas and strategies.

Ultimately, every teacher will use these investigations in ways that make sense for his or her particular style, the particular group of students, and the constraints and supports of a particular school environment. Each unit offers information and guidance for a wide variety of situations, drawn from our collaborations with many teachers and students over many years. Our goal in this book is to help you, a professional educator, implement this curriculum in a way that will give all your students access to mathematical power.

Investigation Format

The opening two pages of each investigation help you get ready for the work that follows.

What Happens This gives a synopsis of each session or block of sessions.

Mathematical Emphasis This lists the most important ideas and processes students will encounter in this investigation.

What to Plan Ahead of Time These lists alert you to materials to gather, sheets to duplicate, transparencies to make, and anything else you need to do before starting.

INVESTIGATION 1

Parts of Squares: Halves, Fourths, and Eighths

What Happens

Session 1: Finding Halves of Crazy Cakes Students divide each of a set of "crazy cakes" in half so two people sharing them will receive the same amount of cake. Since these shapes cannot be readily divided in half based on lines of symmetry, the activity requires that students look for parts of each shape that are equal in area and use visual relationships to make their divisions.

Sessions 2, 3, and 4: Halves, Fourths, and Eighths with Geoboards Students divide a specified area (the square of a geoboard) into halves, fourths, and eighths. Students discuss their solutions and compare various-shaped fourths to show they are the same size. They write justifications for designs partitioned in fourths.

Session 5: Combining Fractions in a Design Students construct ways of dividing a whole into a combination of halves, fourths, and eighths. They make drafts on small dot-paper squares, then copy a favorite onto a large square. After finishing this large square, students write equations that reflect the relationships their designs illustrate.

Mathematical Emphasis

■ Understanding that equal fractions of a whole have the same area

■ Understanding that equal parts of shapes are not necessarily congruent—that is, they may have different shapes

■ Understanding that cutting and pasting shapes conserves their area

■ Becoming familiar with relationships among halves, fourths, and eighths

What to Plan Ahead of Time

Materials

■ Rulers: 1 per pair (all sessions)

■ Scissors: 1 per pair (all sessions)

■ Crayons or markers (all sessions)

■ Geoboards with rubber bands in assorted colors: 1 per pair (Sessions 2–4)

■ Glue sticks: 1 per pair (all sessions)

■ Small stick-on notes: several per student (Sessions 2–4)

■ Overhead projector, transparencies, and pens (Sessions 1–4)

Other Preparation

■ Duplicate student sheets (located at the end of this unit) in the following quantities. If you have Student Activity Booklets, copy only the items marked with an asterisk, including any transparencies needed.

For Session 1
Student Sheet 1, Crazy Cakes for Two (p. 61): 1–2 per student and 1 overhead transparency*

For Sessions 2–4
Student Sheet 2, Dot-Paper Squares (p. 62): 3–4 per student and 3 overhead transparencies*

Student Sheet 3, Proving Fractional Parts (p. 63): 1 per student (optional)

Student Sheet 4, Squares for a Quilt of Fourths (p. 64): 2 per student

Student Sheet 5, A Favorite Fourth (p. 65): 1 per student (homework)

Family letter* (p. 60): 1 per student. Remember to sign it before copying.

For Session 5
Student Sheet 2, Dot-Paper Squares (p. 62): 1–2 per student

Student Sheet 6, Large Dot Square for Combining Fractions (p. 66): 1–2 per student

■ Work out the examples on Student Sheet 1 for yourself before class and read the **Teacher Note**, Strategies for Dividing Crazy Cakes (p. 6) (Session 1).

■ If you plan to provide folders in which students will save their work for the entire unit, prepare these for distribution during Session 1.

Sessions Within an investigation, the activities are organized by class session, a session being at least a one-hour math class. Sessions are numbered consecutively through an investigation. Often several sessions are grouped together, presenting a block of activities with a single major focus.

When you find a block of sessions presented together—for example, Sessions 1, 2, and 3—read through the entire block first to understand the overall flow and sequence of the activities. Make some preliminary decisions about how you will divide the activities into three sessions for your class, based on what you know about your students. You may need to modify your initial plans as you progress through the activities, and you may want to make notes in the margins of the pages as reminders for the next time you use the unit.

Be sure to read the Session Follow-Up section at the end of the session block to see what homework assignments and extensions are suggested as you make your initial plans.

While you may be used to a curriculum that tells you exactly what each class session should cover, we have found that the teacher is in a better position to make these decisions. Each unit is flexible and may be handled somewhat differently by every teacher. While we provide guidance for how many sessions a particular group of activities is likely to need, we want you to be active in determining an appropriate pace and the best transition points for your class. It is not unusual for a teacher to spend more or less time than is proposed for the activities.

Ten-Minute Math At the beginning of some sessions, you will find Ten-Minute Math activities. These are designed to be used in tandem with the investigations, but not during the math hour. Rather, we hope you will do them whenever you have a spare 10 minutes—maybe before lunch or recess, or at the end of the day.

Ten-Minute Math offers practice in key concepts, but not always those being covered in the unit. For example, in a unit on using data, Ten-Minute Math might revisit geometric activities done earlier in the year. Complete directions for the suggested activities are included at the end of each unit.

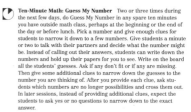

Activities The activities include pair and small-group work, individual tasks, and whole-class discussions. In any case, students are seated together, talking and sharing ideas during all work times. Students most often work cooperatively, although each student may record work individually.

Choice Time In some units, some sessions are structured with activity choices. In these cases, students may work simultaneously on different activities focused on the same mathematical ideas. Students choose which activities they want to do, and they cycle through them.

You will need to decide how to set up and introduce these activities and how to let students make their choices. Some teachers present them as station activities, in different parts of the room. Some list the choices on the board as reminders or have students keep their own lists.

Extensions Sometimes in Session Follow-Up, you will find suggested extension activities. These are opportunities for some or all students to explore a topic in greater depth or in a different context. They are not designed for "fast" students; mathematics is a multifaceted discipline, and different students will want to go further in different investigations. Look for and encourage the sparks of interest and enthusiasm you see in your students, and use the extensions to help them pursue these interests.

Excursions Some of the *Investigations* units include excursions—blocks of activities that could be omitted without harming the integrity of the unit. This is one way of dealing with the great depth and variety of elementary mathematics—much more than a class has time to explore in any one year. Excursions give you the flexibility to make different choices from year to year, doing the excursion in one unit this time, and next year trying another excursion.

Tips for the Linguistically Diverse Classroom At strategic points in each unit, you will find concrete suggestions for simple modifications of the teaching strategies to encourage the participation of all students. Many of these tips offer alternative ways to elicit critical thinking from students at varying levels of English proficiency, as well as from other students who find it difficult to verbalize their thinking.

The tips are supported by suggestions for specific vocabulary work to help ensure that all students can participate fully in the investigations. The Preview for the Linguistically Diverse Classroom (p. I-20) lists important words that are assumed as part of the working vocabulary of the unit. Second-language learners will need to become familiar with these words in order to understand the problems and activities they will be doing. These terms can be incorporated into students' second-language work before or during the unit. Activities that can be used to present the words are found in the appendix, Vocabulary Support for Second-Language Learners (p. 57). In addition, ideas for making connections to students' language and cultures, included on the Preview page, help the class explore the unit's concepts from a multicultural perspective.

Materials

A complete list of the materials needed for teaching this unit is found on p. I-16. Some of these materials are available in kits for the *Investigations* curriculum. Individual items can also be purchased from school supply dealers.

Classroom Materials In an active mathematics classroom, certain basic materials should be available at all times: interlocking cubes, pencils, unlined paper, graph paper, calculators, things to count with, and measuring tools. Some activities in this curriculum require scissors and glue sticks or tape. Stick-on notes and large paper are also useful materials throughout.

So that students can independently get what they need at any time, they should know where these materials are kept, how they are stored, and how they are to be returned to the storage area. For example, interlocking cubes are best stored in towers of ten; then, whatever the activity, they should be returned to storage in groups of ten at the end of the hour. You'll find that establishing such routines at the beginning of the year is well worth the time and effort.

Technology Calculators are used throughout *Investigations.* Many of the units recommend that you have at least one calculator for each pair. You will find calculator activities, plus Teacher Notes discussing this important mathematical tool, in an early unit at each grade level. It is assumed that calculators will be readily available for student use.

Computer activities at grade 4 use a software program that was developed especially for the *Investigations* curriculum. The program *Geo-Logo*™ is used for activities in the 2-D Geometry unit, *Sunken Ships and Grid Patterns,* where students explore coordinate graphing systems, the use of negative numbers to represent locations in space, and the properties of geometric figures.

How you use the computer activities depends on the number of computers you have available. Suggestions are offered in the geometry units for how to organize different types of computer environments.

Children's Literature Each unit offers a list of suggested children's literature (p. I-16) that can be used to support the mathematical ideas in the unit. Sometimes an activity is based on a specific children's book, with suggestions for substitutions where practical. While such activities can be adapted and taught without the book, the literature offers a rich introduction and should be used whenever possible.

Student Sheets and Teaching Resources Student recording sheets and other teaching tools needed for both class and homework are provided as reproducible blackline masters at the end of each unit. They are also available as Student Activity Booklets. These booklets contain all the sheets each student will need for individual work, freeing you from extensive copying (although you may need or want to copy the occasional teaching resource on transparency film or card stock, or make extra copies of a student sheet).

We think it's important that students find their own ways of organizing and recording their work. They need to learn how to explain their thinking with both drawings and written words, and how to organize their results so someone else can under-

---

Name _____ Date _____

Student Sheet 3

Proving Fractional Parts

1. Prove that this square is divided into halves.

2. Prove that this square is divided into fourths.

3. Prove that these two shapes have equal area.

© Dale Seymour Publications®   63   *Investigation 1 • Sessions 2–4 • Different Shapes, Equal Pieces*

---

stand them. For this reason, we deliberately do not provide student sheets for every activity. Regardless of the form in which students do their work, we recommend that they keep a mathematics notebook or folder so that their work is always available for reference.

Homework In *Investigations,* homework is an extension of classroom work. Sometimes it offers review and practice of work done in class, sometimes preparation for upcoming activities, and sometimes numerical practice that revisits work in earlier units. Homework plays a role both in supporting students' learning and in helping inform families about the ways in which students in this curriculum work with mathematical ideas.

Depending on your school's homework policies and your own judgment, you may want to assign more homework than is suggested in the units. For this purpose you might use the practice pages, included as blackline masters at the end of this unit, to give students additional work with numbers.

For some homework assignments, you will want to adapt the activity to meet the needs of a variety of students in your class: those with special needs, those ready for more challenge, and second-language learners. You might change the numbers in a problem, make the activity more or less complex, or go through a sample activity with those who need extra help. You can modify any student sheet for either homework or class use. In particular, making numbers in a problem smaller or larger can make the same basic activity appropriate for a wider range of students.

Another issue to consider is how to handle the homework that students bring back to class—how to recognize the work they have done at home without spending too much time on it. Some teachers hold a short group discussion of different approaches to the assignment; others ask students to share and discuss their work with a neighbor, or post the homework around the room and give students time to tour it briefly. If you want to keep track of homework students bring in, be sure it ends up in a designated place.

Investigations at Home It is a good idea to make your policy on homework explicit to both students and their families when you begin teaching with *Investigations*. How frequently will you be assigning homework? When do you expect homework to be completed and brought back to school? What are your goals in assigning homework? How independent should families expect their children to be? What should the parent's or guardian's role be? The more explicit you can be about your expectations, the better the homework experience will be for everyone.

Investigations at Home (a booklet available separately for each unit, to send home with students) gives you a way to communicate with families about the work students are doing in class. This booklet includes a brief description of every session, a list of the mathematics content emphasized in each investigation, and a discussion of each homework assignment to help families more effectively support their children. Whether or not you are using the *Investigations* at Home booklets, we expect you to make your own choices about home-

work assignments. Feel free to omit any and to add extra ones you think are appropriate.

Family Letter A letter that you can send home to students' families is included with the blackline masters for each unit. Families need to be informed about the mathematics work in your classroom; they should be encouraged to participate in and support their children's work. A reminder to send home the letter for each unit appears in one of the early investigations. These letters are also available separately in Spanish, Vietnamese, Cantonese, Hmong, and Cambodian.

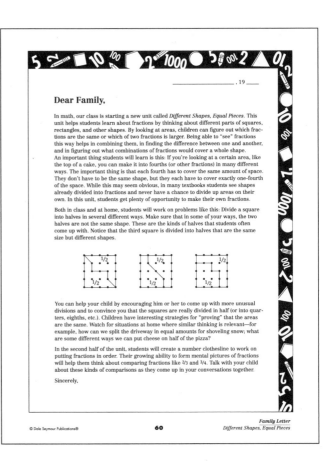

Help for You, the Teacher

Because we believe strongly that a new curriculum must help teachers think in new ways about mathematics and about their students' mathematical thinking processes, we have included a great deal of material to help you learn more about both.

About the Mathematics in This Unit This introductory section (p. I-17) summarizes the critical information about the mathematics you will be teaching. It describes the unit's central mathematical ideas and how students will encounter them through the unit's activities.

Teacher Notes These reference notes provide practical information about the mathematics you are teaching and about our experience with how students learn. Many of the notes were written in response to actual questions from teachers, or to discuss important things we saw happening in the field-test classrooms. Some teachers like to read them all before starting the unit, then review them as they come up in particular investigations.

Dialogue Boxes Sample dialogues demonstrate how students typically express their mathematical ideas, what issues and confusions arise in their thinking, and how some teachers have guided class discussions.

These dialogues are based on the extensive classroom testing of this curriculum; many are word-for-word transcriptions of recorded class discussions. They are not always easy reading; sometimes it may take some effort to unravel what the students are trying to say. But this is the value of these dialogues; they offer good clues to how your students may develop and express their approaches and strategies, helping you prepare for your own class discussions.

Where to Start You may not have time to read everything the first time you use this unit. As a first-time user, you will likely focus on understanding the activities and working them out with your students. Read completely through each investigation before starting to present it. Also read those sections listed in the Contents under the heading Where to Start (p. vi).

Teacher Note ⟩ *Problems with Wholes*

When students are trying to work with fractions both under and over 1 at the same time, they sometimes get confused about what to think of as the whole. In representing a number over 1, for example, they may try to represent the ratio within a single whole. For example, Lesley Ann drew 4/3 like this:

Lesley Ann's 4/3

Lesley Ann: Well, I did 4/3's. And I had two pieces stuck together.

Here Lesley Ann was stumped by the need to have four pieces shaded when thirds only provide three in a single whole. Her solution was to combine two wholes to get enough thirds. Had she kept the two wholes separate, her solution would have been correct.

Some students make more wholes than necessary, rather than fewer. Joey represented 4/3 like this:

Joey's 4/3

Here, Joey may have been thinking about creating four squares, each showing 1/3, for a total of four-thirds. Again, this solution is correct, but confusing. He did not realize he could combine three of the thirds into a whole.

Another example is Luisa's rendition of 1/5.

Luisa's 1/5

It is not clear whether Luisa means to have one out of five sections colored (if you don't count the uncolored half of the third square), or if she means to represent the numerator by the one colored section and the denominator by the five uncolored sections. Neither of these represents one-fifth of one.

These problems do not usually emerge when students are working only with fractions under 1, but these kinds of responses may uncover students' lack of clarity about the role of wholes in representing fractions.

44 ▪ *Investigation 3: Ordering Fractions*

▪ D I A L O G U E ▪ B O X ▪

How Do You Know It's Half?

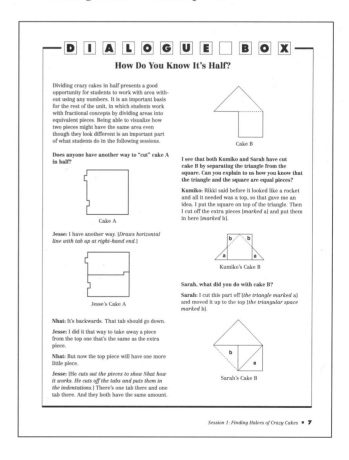

Dividing crazy cakes in half presents a good opportunity for students to work with area without using any numbers. It is an important basis for the rest of the unit, in which students work with fractional concepts by dividing areas into equivalent pieces. Being able to visualize how two pieces might have the same area even though they look different is an important part of what students do in the following sessions.

Does anyone have another way to "cut" cake A in half?

Cake A

Jesse: I have another way. [*Draws horizontal line with tab up at right-hand end.*]

Jesse's Cake A

Nhat: It's backwards. That tab should go down.

Jesse: I did it that way to take away a piece from the top one that's the same as the extra piece.

Nhat: But now the top piece will have one more little piece.

Jesse: [*He cuts out the pieces to show Nhat how it works. He cuts off the tabs and puts them in the indentations.*] There's one tab there and one tab there. And they both have the same amount.

Cake B

I see that both Kumiko and Sarah have cut cake B by separating the triangle from the square. Can you explain to us how you know that the triangle and the square are equal pieces?

Kumiko: Rikki said before it looked like a rocket and all it needed was a top, so that gave me an idea. I put the square on top of the triangle. Then I cut off the extra pieces [*marked a*] and put them in here [*marked b*].

Kumiko's Cake B

Sarah, what did you do with cake B?

Sarah: I cut this part off [*the triangle marked a*] and moved it up to the top [*the triangular space marked b*].

Sarah's Cake B

Session 1: Finding Halves of Crazy Cakes ▪ **7**

The *Investigations* curriculum incorporates the use of two forms of technology in the classroom: calculators and computers. Calculators are assumed to be standard classroom materials, available for student use in any unit. Computers are explicitly linked to one or more units at each grade level; they are used with the unit on 2-D geometry at each grade, as well as with some of the units on measuring, data, and changes.

Using Calculators

In this curriculum, calculators are considered tools for doing mathematics, similar to pattern blocks or interlocking cubes. Just as with other tools, students must learn both *how* to use calculators correctly and *when* they are appropriate to use. This knowledge is crucial for daily life, as calculators are now a standard way of handling numerical operations, both at work and at home.

Using a calculator correctly is not a simple task; it depends on a good knowledge of the four operations and of the number system, so that students can select suitable calculations and also determine what a reasonable result would be. These skills are the basis of any work with numbers, whether or not a calculator is involved.

Unfortunately, calculators are often seen as tools to check computations with, as if other methods are somehow more fallible. Students need to understand that any computational method can be used to check any other; it's just as easy to make a mistake on the calculator as it is to make a mistake on paper or with mental arithmetic. Throughout this curriculum, we encourage students to solve computation problems in more than one way in order to double-check their accuracy. We present mental arithmetic, paper-and-pencil computation, and calculators as three possible approaches.

In this curriculum we also recognize that, despite their importance, calculators are not always appropriate in mathematics instruction. Like any tools, calculators are useful for some tasks, but not for others. You will need to make decisions about when to allow students access to calculators and when to ask that they solve problems without them, so that they can concentrate on other tools and skills. At times when calculators are or are not appropriate for a particular activity, we make specific recommendations. Help your students develop their own sense of which problems they can tackle with their own reasoning and which ones might be better solved with a combination of their own reasoning and the calculator.

Managing calculators in your classroom so that they are a tool, and not a distraction, requires some planning. When calculators are first introduced, students often want to use them for everything, even problems that can be solved quite simply by other methods. However, once the novelty wears off, students are just as interested in developing their own strategies, especially when these strategies are emphasized and valued in the classroom. Over time, students will come to recognize the ease and value of solving problems mentally, with paper and pencil, or with manipulatives, while also understanding the power of the calculator to facilitate work with larger numbers.

Experience shows that if calculators are available only occasionally, students become excited and distracted when they are permitted to use them. They focus on the tool rather than on the mathematics. In order to learn when calculators are appropriate and when they are not, students must have easy access to them and use them routinely in their work.

If you have a calculator for each student, and if you think your students can accept the responsibility, you might allow them to keep their calculators with the rest of their individual materials, at least for the first few weeks of school. Alternatively, you might store them in boxes on a shelf, number each calculator, and assign a corresponding number to each student. This system can give students a sense of ownership while also helping you keep track of the calculators.

Using Computers

Students can use computers to approach and visualize mathematical situations in new ways. The computer allows students to construct and manipulate geometric shapes, see objects move according to rules they specify, and turn, flip, and repeat a pattern.

This curriculum calls for computers in units where they are a particularly effective tool for learning mathematics content. One unit on 2-D geometry at each of the grades 3–5 includes a core of activities that rely on access to computers, either in the classroom or in a lab. Other units on geometry, measurement, data, and changes include computer activities, but can be taught without them. In these units, however, students' experience is greatly enhanced by computer use.

The following list outlines the recommended use of computers in this curriculum:

Grade 1
Unit: *Survey Questions and Secret Rules*
   (Collecting and Sorting Data)
Software: Tabletop, Jr.
Source: Broderbund

Unit: *Quilt Squares and Block Towns*
   (2-D and 3-D Geometry)
Software: *Shapes*
Source: provided with the unit

Grade 2
Unit: *Mathematical Thinking at Grade 2*
   (Introduction)
Software: *Shapes*
Source: provided with the unit

Unit: *Shapes, Halves, and Symmetry*
   (Geometry and Fractions)
Software: *Shapes*
Source: provided with the unit

Unit: *How Long? How Far?* (Measuring)
Software: *Geo-Logo*
Source: provided with the unit

Grade 3
Unit: *Flips, Turns, and Area* (2-D Geometry)
Software: *Tumbling Tetrominoes*
Source: provided with the unit

Unit: *Turtle Paths* (2-D Geometry)
Software: *Geo-Logo*
Source: provided with the unit

Grade 4
Unit: *Sunken Ships and Grid Patterns*
   (2-D Geometry)
Software: *Geo-Logo*
Source: provided with the unit

Grade 5
Unit: *Picturing Polygons* (2-D Geometry)
Software: *Geo-Logo*
Source: provided with the unit

Unit: *Patterns of Change* (Tables and Graphs)
Software: *Trips*
Source: provided with the unit

Unit: *Data: Kids, Cats, and Ads* (Statistics)
Software: Tabletop, Sr.
Source: Broderbund

The software provided with the *Investigations* units uses the power of the computer to help students explore mathematical ideas and relationships that cannot be explored in the same way with physical materials. With the *Shapes* (grades 1–2) and *Tumbling Tetrominoes* (grade 3) software, students explore symmetry, pattern, rotation and reflection, area, and characteristics of 2-D shapes. With the *Geo-Logo* software (grades 3–5), students investigate rotations and reflections, coordinate geometry, the properties of 2-D shapes, and angles. The *Trips* software (grade 5) is a mathematical exploration of motion in which students run experiments and interpret data presented in graphs and tables.

We suggest that students work in pairs on the computer; this not only maximizes computer resources but also encourages students to consult, monitor, and teach one another. Generally, more than two students at one computer find it difficult to share. Managing access to computers is an issue for every classroom. The curriculum gives you explicit support for setting up a system. The units are structured on the assumption that you have enough computers for half your students to work on the machines in pairs at one time. If you do not have access to that many computers, suggestions are made for structuring class time to use the unit with five to eight computers, or even with fewer than five.

Assessment plays a critical role in teaching and learning, and it is an integral part of the *Investigations* curriculum. For a teacher using these units, assessment is an ongoing process. You observe students' discussions and explanations of their strategies on a daily basis and examine their work as it evolves. While students are busy recording and representing their work, working on projects, sharing with partners, and playing mathematical games, you have many opportunities to observe their mathematical thinking. What you learn through observation guides your decisions about how to proceed. In any of the units, you will repeatedly consider questions like these:

- Do students come up with their own strategies for solving problems, or do they expect others to tell them what to do? What do their strategies reveal about their mathematical understanding?

- Do students understand that there are different strategies for solving problems? Do they articulate their strategies and try to understand other students' strategies?

- How effectively do students use materials as tools to help with their mathematical work?

- Do students have effective ideas for keeping track of and recording their work? Does keeping track of and recording their work seem difficult for them?

You will need to develop a comfortable and efficient system for recording and keeping track of your observations. Some teachers keep a clipboard handy and jot notes on a class list or on adhesive labels that are later transferred to student files. Others keep loose-leaf notebooks with a page for each student and make weekly notes about what they have observed in class.

Assessment Tools in the Unit

With the activities in each unit, you will find questions to guide your thinking while observing the students at work. You will also find two built-in assessment tools: Teacher Checkpoints and embedded Assessment activities.

Teacher Checkpoints The designated Teacher Checkpoints in each unit offer a time to "check in" with individual students, watch them at work, and ask questions that illuminate how they are thinking.

At first it may be hard to know what to look for, hard to know what kinds of questions to ask. Students may be reluctant to talk; they may not be accustomed to having the teacher ask them about their work, or they may not know how to explain their thinking. Two important ingredients of this process are asking students open-ended questions about their work and showing genuine interest in how they are approaching the task. When students see that you are interested in their thinking and are counting on them to come up with their own ways of solving problems, they may surprise you with the depth of their understanding.

Teacher Checkpoints also give you the chance to pause in the teaching sequence and reflect on how your class is doing overall. Think about whether you need to adjust your pacing: Are most students fluent with strategies for solving a particular kind of problem? Are they just starting to formulate good strategies? Or are they still struggling with how to start? Depending on what you see as the students work, you may want to spend more time on similar problems, change some of the problems to use smaller numbers, move quickly to more challenging material, modify subsequent activities for some students, work on particular ideas with a small group, or pair students who have good strategies with those who are having more difficulty.

Embedded Assessment Activities Assessment activities embedded in each unit will help you examine specific pieces of student work, figure out what it means, and provide feedback. From the students' point of view, these assessment activities are no different from any others. Each is a learning experience in and of itself, as well as an opportunity for you to gather evidence about students' mathematical understanding.

The embedded assessment activities sometimes involve writing and reflecting; at other times, a discussion or brief interaction between student and teacher; and in still other instances, the creation and explanation of a product. In most cases, the assessments require that students *show* what they did, *write* or *talk* about it, or do both. Having to explain how they worked through a problem helps students be more focused and clear in their mathematical thinking. It also helps them realize that doing mathematics is a process that may involve tentative starts, revising one's approach, taking different paths, and working through ideas.

Teachers often find the hardest part of assessment to be interpreting their students' work. We provide guidelines to help with that interpretation. If you have used a process approach to teaching writing, the assessment in *Investigations* will seem familiar. For many of the assessment activities, a Teacher Note provides examples of student work and a commentary on what it indicates about student thinking.

Documentation of Student Growth

To form an overall picture of mathematical progress, it is important to document each student's work in journals, notebooks, or portfolios. The choice is largely a matter of personal preference; some teachers have students keep a notebook or folder for each unit, while others prefer one mathematics notebook, or a portfolio of selected work for the entire year. The final activity in each *Investigations* unit, called Choosing Student Work to Save, helps you and the students select representative samples for a record of their work.

This kind of regular documentation helps you synthesize information about each student as a mathematical learner. From different pieces of evidence, you can put together the big picture. This synthesis will be invaluable in thinking about where to go next with a particular child, deciding where more work is needed, or explaining to parents (or other teachers) how a child is doing.

If you use portfolios, you need to collect a good balance of work, yet avoid being swamped with an overwhelming amount of paper. Following are some tips for effective portfolios:

- Collect a representative sample of work, including some pieces that students themselves select for inclusion in the portfolio. There should be just a few pieces for each unit, showing different kinds of work—some assignments that involve writing, as well as some that do not.

- If students do not date their work, do so yourself so that you can reconstruct the order in which pieces were done.

- Include your reflections on the work. When you are looking back over the whole year, such comments are reminders of what seemed especially interesting about a particular piece; they can also be helpful to other teachers and to parents. Older students should be encouraged to write their own reflections about their work.

Assessment Overview

There are two places to turn for a preview of the assessment opportunities in each *Investigations* unit. The Assessment Resources column in the unit Overview Chart (pp. I-13–I-15) identifies the Teacher Checkpoints and Assessment activities embedded in each investigation, guidelines for observing the students that appear within classroom activities, and any Teacher Notes and Dialogue Boxes that explain what to look for and what types of student responses you might expect to see in your classroom. Additionally, the section About the Assessment in This Unit (p. I-18) gives you a detailed list of questions for each investigation, keyed to the mathematical emphases, to help you observe student growth.

Depending on your situation, you may want to provide additional assessment opportunities. Most of the investigations lend themselves to more frequent assessment, simply by having students do more writing and recording while they are working.

Different Shapes, Equal Pieces

Content of This Unit Students explore fractions by dividing square areas into halves, fourths, and eighths and rectangular areas into thirds, sixths, and twelfths. To work on ordering fractions, including those greater than 1, students make a deck of fraction cards with fractions between 0 and 3 and order subsets of them on a single number line. They play Fish and Capture Fractions to practice identifying equivalent fractions and ordering fractions, respectively.

Connections with Other Units In the third grade unit *Fair Shares*, students partition rectangular "brownies" into fair shares and work with pattern blocks. If your students have had limited experience with visual models for fractions, do the *Fair Shares* unit now and postpone this unit to later in the year or fifth grade. In the fourth grade unit *Three out of Four Like Spaghetti*, your students will make fraction rulers and work with fractions of a group. In the fifth grade fractions unit, students will continue learning about order and equivalence relationships among fractions while working with the ruler, or number line, model.

If your school is not using the full-year curriculum, this unit can also be used successfully at Grade 5 or 6, depending on the needs of your students.

Investigations Curriculum ■ Suggested Grade 4 Sequence

Mathematical Thinking at Grade 4 (Introduction)

Arrays and Shares (Multiplication and Division)

Seeing Solids and Silhouettes (3-D Geometry)

Landmarks in the Thousands (The Number System)

▶ *Different Shapes, Equal Pieces* (Fractions and Area)

The Shape of the Data (Statistics)

Money, Miles, and Large Numbers (Addition and Subtraction)

Changes Over Time (Graphs)

Packages and Groups (Multiplication and Division)

Sunken Ships and Grid Patterns (2-D Geometry)

Three out of Four Like Spaghetti (Data and Fractions)

Investigation 1 ▪ Parts of Squares: Halves, Fourths, and Eighths

Class Sessions	Activities	Pacing
Session 1 (p. 4) FINDING HALVES OF CRAZY CAKES	Crazy Cakes for Two Extension: Inventing Crazy Cakes	minimum 1 hr
Sessions 2, 3, and 4 (p. 8) HALVES, FOURTHS, AND EIGHTHS WITH GEOBOARDS	Halves on the Geoboard and Dot Paper Fourths and Eighths A Page of Favorite Fourths Equal Fourths? Teacher Checkpoint: Writing Proofs for Fractional Parts Making a Fourths Quilt Homework: Dot-Paper Squares Homework: Dividing into Fourths Homework: A Favorite Fourth	minimum 3 hr
Session 5 (p. 19) COMBINING FRACTIONS IN A DESIGN	Combining Halves, Fourths, and Eighths Writing Fraction Relationships Homework: Large Dot Square for Combining Fractions	minimum 1 hr

◕ **Ten-Minute Math** ▪ **Guess My Number**

Mathematical Emphasis

- Understanding that equal fractions of a whole have the same area

- Understanding that equal parts of shapes are not necessarily congruent—that is, they may have different shapes

- Understanding that cutting and pasting shapes conserves their area

- Becoming familiar with relationships among halves, fourths, and eighths

Assessment Resources

Strategies for Dividing Crazy Cakes (Teacher Note, p. 6)

How Do You Know It's Half? (Dialogue Box, p. 7)

Observing the Students (p. 11)

Teacher Checkpoint: Writing Proofs for Fractional Parts (p. 15)

Students' Work on Fourths and Eighths (Teacher Note, p. 16)

Equal Fourths? (Teacher Note, p. 17)

Students Write About Fractions (Teacher Note, p. 18)

Materials

Rulers

Scissors

Crayons or markers

Geoboards with rubber bands in assorted colors

Glue sticks

Small stick-on notes

Overhead projector, transparencies, and pens

Student Sheets 1–6

Family letter

Investigation 2 ▪ Parts of Rectangles: Thirds, Sixths, and Twelfths

Class Sessions	Activities	Pacing
Sessions 1 and 2 (p. 24) THIRDS, SIXTHS, AND TWELFTHS	Working with Thirds and Sixths A Page of Favorite Thirds and Sixths Homework: Dot-Paper Rectangles Homework: Thirds and Sixths	minimum 2 hr
Session 3 (p. 29) MORE FRACTION DESIGNS	Assessment: Proving Thirds and Sixths Making a Combined Design Homework: Large Dot Rectangle for Combining Fractions Extension: Writing Equations Equal to 1 Extension: Making Fractional Flags	minimum 1 hr
Session 4 (p. 33) WORKING WITH $2/3$, $3/4$, $5/6$, AND $7/8$	Making Colored Squares Teacher Checkpoint: Agree or Disagree? Homework: Writing About a Colored-Square Design	minimum 1 hr

◔ **Ten-Minute Math** ▪ **Guess My Number**

Mathematical Emphasis

- Knowing that equal fractions of different-sized wholes will be different in area

- Becoming familiar with relationships among thirds, sixths, and twelfths

- Using different combinations to make a whole

- Comparing fractions that have "one piece missing"

- Working with fractions that have numerators larger than one

Assessment Resources

A Strategy for Finding Interesting Thirds (Teacher Note, p. 28)

Assessment: Proving Thirds and Sixths (p. 29)

Assessment: Proving Thirds and Sixths (Teacher Note, p. 32)

Teacher Checkpoint: Agree or Disagree? (p. 35)

Accurate Drawings or Accurate Knowledge? (Teacher Note, p. 37)

Materials

Rulers

Crayons or markers

Small stick-on notes

Scissors

Colored paper

Glue sticks

Overhead projector, transparencies, and pens

Geoboards

Calculators

Student Sheets 7–13

Teaching resource sheet

Investigation 3 ▪ Ordering Fractions

Class Sessions	Activities	Pacing
Sessions 1 and 2 (p. 40) MAKING FRACTION CARDS	Making Fraction Cards Recognizing Equivalent Fractions Playing Fraction Fish Homework: Playing Fraction Fish	minimum 2 hr
Session 3 (p. 46) ORDERING FRACTIONS WITH RESPECT TO LANDMARKS	Groups Order Fractions with Respect to Landmarks Homework: Fractions in Containers	minimum 1 hr
Sessions 4 and 5 (p. 49) MAKING A FRACTION NUMBER LINE	Playing Capture Fractions Making a Fraction Number Line Assessment: Comparing Fractions Choosing Student Work to Save Homework: Playing Capture Fractions	minimum 2 hr

◓ Ten-Minute Math ▪ Guess My Number

Mathematical Emphasis

- Comparing any fraction to the land-marks 0, 1/2, 1, and 2

- Using both numerical reasoning and area to order fractions

- Using the size of the numerator to compare fractions that have the same denominator

- Using the size of the denominator to compare fractions with the same numerator

- Comparing fractions greater than 1 with fractions less than or equal to 1

- Understanding that fractions "missing one piece" are ordered inversely to the size of the missing piece

- Identifying equivalent fractions

Assessment Resources

Problems with Wholes (Teacher Note, p. 44)

Visualizing Equivalent Fractions (Teacher Note, p. 45)

Comparing Fractions to 1/2 (Teacher Note, p. 48)

Assessment: Comparing Fractions (p. 50)

Choosing Student Work to Save (p. 51)

Strategies for Comparing Fractions (Teacher Note, p. 52)

Assessment: Comparing Fractions (Teacher Note, p. 53)

Materials

Oak tag

Crayons or markers

Overhead projector, transparencies, and pens

Scissors

Glue sticks

Yarn or string

Paper clips

Student Sheets 14–15

Teaching resource sheets

Following are the basic materials needed for the activities in this unit. Many of the items can be purchased from the publisher, either individually or in the Teacher Resource Package and the Student Materials Kit for grade 4. Detailed information is available on the *Investigations* order form. To obtain this form, call toll-free 1-800-872-1100 and ask for a Dale Seymour customer service representative.

Overhead projector, transparencies, and pens (important for this unit)

Rulers: 1 per pair of students

Scissors: 1 per pair of students

Crayons or markers

Geoboards with rubber bands in assorted colors: 1 per pair of students

Glue sticks: 1 per pair of students

Oak tag for fraction cards—15 letter-size sheets per deck: 1 class deck and 1 deck per group of 4 students (use colored oak tag and a different color for each deck, if possible)

Oak tag for landmark cards—2 letter-size sheets per set: 2 class sets and 1 set per group of 4 students

Small stick-on notes

Colored paper (optional)

Yarn or string: 2 pieces (about 15 feet each)

Paper clips

Calculators: 1 per pair of students (Ten-Minute Math)

Tape

The following materials are provided at the end of this unit as blackline masters. A Student Activity Booklet containing all student sheets and teaching resources needed for individual work is available.

Family Letter (p. 60)

Student Sheets 1–15 (p. 61)

Teaching Resources:

How Much Is Colored? (p. 75)

Fractions for Fraction Cards (p. 79)

Blank Wholes for Fraction Cards (p. 80)

How to Play Fraction Fish (p. 81)

Fraction Cards for Playing Fraction Fish (p. 82)

Table for Grouping Fractions Between Landmarks (p. 83)

How to Play Capture Fractions (p. 84)

Practice Pages (p. 85)

Related Children's Literature

Ernst, Lisa Campbell. *Sam Johnson and the Blue Ribbon Quilt*. New York: Lothrop, Lee and Shepard, 1983.

Leedy, Loreen. *Fraction Action*. New York: Holiday House, 1994.

Wilder, Laura Ingalls. *Little House in the Big Woods* (Chapter 10). New York: Harper and Row, 1932.

One thing that complicates learning about fractions is that a simple fraction such as 3/4 can refer to several kinds of situations, part of the area of a shape (six of eight parts of a square), part of a group of things (75 dogs out of a total of 100 pets), part of a length (three-quarters of the distance from the door to the window), or a rate (4 raffle tickets for 3 dollars). Each of these situations provides a model that allows students to visualize fractions.

This unit, *Different Shapes, Equal Pieces*, concentrates on an area model for fractions in which fractions less than one are described as portions of an area such as one square or one rectangle. Using an area model for fractions helps emphasize some central concepts about fractions:

- Fractional parts of a whole are equal parts. Understanding this statement entails both (1) recognizing equal areas as fractional parts when an area is already divided and (2) being able to partition an area into fractional parts by dividing the area equally.

- A certain fraction represents different sizes if the wholes of which it is part are different. One-quarter of the area of a basketball court is different from one-quarter of the area of a football field.

- Equal parts of shapes are not necessarily congruent. The two halves or four quarters of a square may look different but can still be equal in area. A particular half acre of land may be shaped quite differently from some other half acre, but both can still be exactly half of an acre.

- Two fractions (relative to the same unit whole) can be compared. Just as we can compare two areas and decide that one is bigger or both are the same size, we can compare two fractions by comparing the areas they represent.

Students not only develop an understanding of fractions in this unit but also learn a great deal about area. Area is approached through visualization rather than formulas. Areas can often be compared by cutting and moving portions of shapes to see if they cover one another. For example, it is possible to show that a rectangle can be divided into two equal triangles by drawing a diagonal in the rectangle, cutting out the triangles, and physically comparing them. This manipulation provides a visual connection to the formula for the area of a triangle, $A = 1/2\ bh$, which students will encounter in later years.

This unit also involves comparing fractions using landmarks. While our approach takes advantage of students' visualizing skills, it also relies on reasoning based on the relationships among numbers. For example, 1/2 is larger than 3/7 because half would be 31/2 sevenths and 3/7 is less than 31/2 sevenths. The concept of "landmark," developed with respect to whole numbers, is extended to fractions, and fractions are sometimes compared by noting their distance from a fraction landmark.

Mathematical Emphasis   At the beginning of each investigation, the Mathematical Emphasis section tells you what is most important for students to learn during that investigation. Many of these mathematical understandings and processes are difficult and complex. Students gradually learn more and more about each idea over many years of schooling. Individual students will begin and end the unit with different levels of knowledge and skill, but all will gain greater knowledge about relationships among common fractions and about ways to compare areas.

Throughout the *Investigations* curriculum, there are many opportunities for ongoing daily assessment as you observe, listen to, and interact with students at work. In this unit, you will find two Teacher Checkpoints:

Investigation 1, Sessions 2–4
Writing Proofs for Fractional Parts (p. 15)

Investigation 2, Session 4
Agree or Disagree? (p. 35)

This unit also has two embedded assessment activities:

Investigation 2, Session 3
Proving Thirds and Sixths (p. 29)

Investigation 3, Sessions 4–5
Comparing Fractions (p. 50)

In addition, you can use almost any activity in this unit to assess your students' needs and strengths. Listed below are questions to help you focus your observation in each investigation. You may want to keep track of your observations for each student to help you plan your curriculum and monitor students' growth. Suggestions for documenting student growth can be found in the section About Assessment (p. I-10).

Investigation 1: Parts of Squares: Halves, Fourths, and Eighths

■ How do students divide a whole into equal parts (halves, fourths, eighths)? Do they know that the parts must be equal in area but not necessarily congruent? Do they know that equal parts can have very different shapes? Do they know that the fraction depends on the number of equal parts rather than the number of units in each part (for example, one-third is one of three equal parts, not necessarily a part with three units of area)?

■ How do students prove the equivalence of area? Do students visually cut and paste shapes to "see" if the parts are equal? Do they count the squares (instead of the geoboard pins) to find the area? How do they count parts of squares? Can they prove equivalence in more than one way?

■ How do students relate halves, fourths, and eighths? Do they recognize equivalent fractions ($1/2$, $2/4$, $4/8$)? Do they see fourths as halves of halves? eighths as halves of fourths? How do they see and use relationships among these fractions to reason and explain solutions to problems?

Investigation 2: Parts of Rectangles: Thirds, Sixths, and Twelfths

■ How do students divide a different size whole into equal parts? Do they realize that the size of the whole affects the size of the fraction (half a square of 16 squares is 8; half a rectangle of 24 squares is 12)?

■ How do students relate thirds, sixths, and twelfths? Do they recognize equivalent fractions ($1/3$, $2/6$, $4/12$)? Do they see sixths as halves of thirds? twelfths as halves of sixths? How do they see and use relationships among these fractions to reason and explain solutions to problems? Do they use prior solutions for halves and thirds in their designs of sixths and twelfths?

■ How do students combine different fractions to make a whole? Can they see and explain relationships among fractions within their designs? Do their designs accurately combine to make one whole? How do students use their designs to generate equations with fractions?

■ How do students compare fractions with one piece missing? (For example, $3/4$ is missing one-fourth and $5/6$ is missing one-sixth.) Do they compare the actual size of the missing piece? the size of the existing pieces? the numerators? the denominators? Do they use landmarks and their knowledge of relationships among fractions? Do they realize that to compare two fractions the wholes must be the same size?

■ How do students make sense of fractions with numerators larger than 1? Do they understand that these represent more than one? How do students compare $2/3$ and $3/2$? How do they explain their reasoning and justify their answers?

Investigation 3: Ordering Fractions

- How do students use landmark numbers (0, $\frac{1}{2}$, 1, 2) to compare fractions? Do they consider a fraction's distance from the nearest landmark? Can they sort fractions into categories based on these landmarks?

- How do students order fractions? How do they use numerical reasoning? (For example, $\frac{4}{9}$ is smaller than $\frac{1}{2}$ because $2 \times \frac{4}{9} = \frac{8}{9}$, which is less than 1.) How do they reason about area to order fractions? Do they use a combination of both?

- How do students compare fractions that have the same denominator? Do they know that the larger the numerator the larger the fraction (for example, $\frac{3}{4}$ is larger than $\frac{2}{4}$)?

- How do students compare fractions with the same numerator? Do they use their knowledge about the size of the pieces (for example, $\frac{2}{3}$ is larger than $\frac{2}{4}$ because thirds are larger than fourths)?

- How do students compare fractions greater than 1 with fractions less than or equal to 1? How do students order fractions with one piece missing? Do they understand that they are ordered inversely to the size of the missing piece (for example, $\frac{2}{3}$ is smaller than $\frac{3}{4}$ because the $\frac{1}{3}$ missing is larger than the $\frac{1}{4}$ missing)?

In the *Investigations* curriculum, mathematical vocabulary is introduced naturally during the activities. We don't ask students to learn definitions of new terms; rather, they come to understand such words as *factor* or *area* or *symmetry* by hearing them used frequently in discussion as they investigate new concepts. This approach is compatible with current theories of second-language acquisition, which emphasize the use of new vocabulary in meaningful contexts while students are actively involved with objects, pictures, and physical movement.

Listed below are some key words used in this unit that will not be new to most English speakers at this age level, but may be unfamiliar to students with limited English proficiency. You will want to spend additional time working on these words with your students who are learning English. If your students are working with a second-language teacher, you might enlist your colleague's aid in familiarizing students with these words, before and during this unit. In the classroom, look for opportunities for students to hear and use these words. Activities you can use to present the words are given in the appendix, Vocabulary Support for Second-Language Learners (p. 57).

cake   In the first activity, students partition areas of "crazy cakes" (polygons with unusual shapes) into halves by dissecting the shapes and moving portions.

flag   As an extension, students design or draw real flags and write about what fraction of the flag is colored each color.

quilt   Students design a nine-square quilt in which each square is divided into fourths in a different way.

Multicultural Extensions for All Students

Whenever possible, encourage students to share words, objects, customs, or any aspects of daily life from their own cultures and backgrounds that are relevant to the activities in this unit. For example:

■ When students are identifying fractions of areas that are colored in flags, they may want to use flags or other national emblems from their family's country of origin.

Investigations

Parts of Squares: Halves, Fourths, and Eighths

What Happens

Session 1: Finding Halves of Crazy Cakes
Students divide each of a set of "crazy cakes" in half so two people sharing them will receive the same amount of cake. Since these shapes cannot be readily divided in half based on lines of symmetry, the activity requires that students look for parts of each shape that are equal in area and use visual relationships to make their divisions.

Sessions 2, 3, and 4: Halves, Fourths, and Eighths with Geoboards Students divide a specified area (the square of a geoboard) into halves, fourths, and eighths. Students discuss their solutions and compare various-shaped fourths to show they are the same size. They write justifications for designs partitioned in fourths.

Session 5: Combining Fractions in a Design
Students construct ways of dividing a whole into a combination of halves, fourths, and eighths. They make drafts on small dot-paper squares, then copy a favorite onto a large square. After finishing this large square, students write equations that reflect the relationships their designs illustrate.

Mathematical Emphasis

■ Understanding that equal fractions of a whole have the same area

■ Understanding that equal parts of shapes are not necessarily congruent—that is, they may have different shapes

■ Understanding that cutting and pasting shapes conserves their area

■ Becoming familiar with relationships among halves, fourths, and eighths

What to Plan Ahead of Time

Materials

- Rulers: 1 per pair (all sessions)
- Scissors: 1 per pair (all sessions)
- Crayons or markers (all sessions)
- Geoboards with rubber bands in assorted colors: 1 per pair (Sessions 2–4)
- Glue sticks: 1 per pair (all sessions)
- Small stick-on notes: several per student (Sessions 2–4)
- Overhead projector, transparencies, and pens (Sessions 1–4)

Other Preparation

- Duplicate student sheets (located at the end of this unit) in the following quantities. If you have Student Activity Booklets, copy only the items marked with an asterisk, including any transparencies needed.

  For Session 1
  Student Sheet 1, Crazy Cakes for Two (p. 61): 1–2 per student and 1 overhead transparency*

  For Sessions 2–4
  Student Sheet 2, Dot-Paper Squares (p. 62): 3–4 per student and 3 overhead transparencies*

  Student Sheet 3, Proving Fractional Parts (p. 63): 1 per student (optional)

  Student Sheet 4, Squares for a Quilt of Fourths (p. 64): 2 per student

  Student Sheet 5, A Favorite Fourth (p. 65): 1 per student (homework)

  Family letter* (p. 60): 1 per student. Remember to sign it before copying.

  For Session 5
  Student Sheet 2, Dot-Paper Squares (p. 62): 1–2 per student

  Student Sheet 6, Large Dot Square for Combining Fractions (p. 66): 1–2 per student

- Work out the examples on Student Sheet 1 for yourself before class and read the **Teacher Note**, Strategies for Dividing Crazy Cakes (p. 6) (Session 1).

- If you plan to provide folders in which students will save their work for the entire unit, prepare these for distribution during Session 1.

Finding Halves of Crazy Cakes

Materials

- Scissors (1 per pair)
- Transparency of Student Sheet 1
- Student Sheet 1 (2 per student)
- Glue sticks (1 per pair)
- Crayons or markers
- Rulers (1 per pair)
- Overhead projector

What Happens

Students each divide a set of "crazy cakes" in half so two people sharing them would receive the same amount of cake. Since these shapes cannot be readily divided in half based on lines of symmetry, the activity requires that students look for parts of each shape that are equal in area and use visual relationships to make their divisions. Their work focuses on:

- understanding that equal fractions of a whole have the same area
- understanding that cutting and pasting shapes conserves their area
- finding halves of a shape

Activity

Crazy Cakes for Two

Draw a copy of example A from Student Sheet 1, Crazy Cakes for Two, on the board, or display it on a transparency if you are using an overhead. You can project the image of example A on the board so that you or a student can draw directly on the board. You may want to make several copies of example A by moving the projector and tracing the image on the board. Tell students that they will find different ways to divide shapes into equal parts in this investigation as a way of learning about fractions such as halves and fourths. You can begin this way:

If this were a cake you had to share evenly between two people, how could you cut it? You need to be able to explain how you know that each person would get the same amount of cake.

Draw or have students draw their solutions on the board. For each idea, ask students to tell you how they know each person would get the same amount of cake. Welcome students' questions and challenges as part of this introduction. Your job is to help students look at the area of each of their "halves" and determine whether they are in fact equal and to help them verbalize the strategies they are using for finding these solutions.

Hand out Student Sheet 1, Crazy Cakes for Two. Encourage students to use cutting, folding, or any other means that helps them prove to themselves and to one another that they have made halves for example A. See the **Teacher Note**, Strategies for Dividing Crazy Cakes (p. 6).

Dividing Shapes in Half   Students work in pairs to find ways to divide fairly each of the crazy cakes on Student Sheet 1. Point out to students that Crazy Cake I is more difficult than the rest. If students would like to have something to show their families as they begin a new unit, each student can create a finished version of Student Sheet 1 that shows with pencils or markers how to "cut" each cake. Make available extra copies of Student Sheet 1 in case they want to cut out the shapes to help them find and prove halves.

Visit student groups as they work and ask them to show you how they know *both people will get the same amount of cake.* They must convince you the two parts are equal. If a student thinks "there's no way" to divide a given shape in half, ask what it is about the shape that makes it "impossible." This can help students think about the areas of parts of the shape in relation to each other.

Proving Halves Are Equal   Once students have had enough time to create "fair shares" of most of the examples on Student Sheet 1, gather the whole class for a discussion of their solutions or, if you prefer, suggest that two or three pairs get together to compare their work and explain their strategies. There are two main goals for this discussion: for students to talk about the thinking that went into their solutions, and for students to see the variety of strategies they can use to help them compare the area in each of their halves for a given shape. If students compare their work in small groups, bring the whole class together briefly to share strategies they learned from one another and to discuss any unresolved disputes. For the whole-class discussion, use an overhead projector or a chalkboard so students can diagram their halves for the class. See the sample strategies and discussion in the **Dialogue Box,** How Do You Know It's Half? (p. 7).

Don't be too concerned about getting through each example on Student Sheet 1 during the discussion. It is more important for students to learn strategies that work in a variety of situations than to learn a "right" way of dividing each particular shape. Take whatever time is needed for students to communicate the different strategies they used and to try out strategies they have learned from others. You might start the discussion by asking a student to show a strategy learned from someone else. Emphasize matching areas, not accuracy in drawing lines or cutting out shapes.

Session 1 Follow-Up

Inventing Crazy Cakes   Students make up their own Crazy Cakes with which they can challenge one another. Before asking another student to cut their cakes into halves, students must be able to do so themselves; they should be able to make halves with a straight line.

 **Extension**

The crazy cakes on Student Sheet 1 will initially challenge many students, but there are ways to approach these examples that will help students build their understanding of area. Example A, for example, can be divided into halves fairly in several ways by focusing on the "bump" and the indentation.

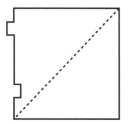 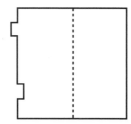

Two correct divisions of example A

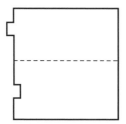

An incorrect division

In the solutions that work, the bump and the indentation (which are the same area) are in the same half. Some students may need to cut out the "bump" and put it in the indentation to convince themselves that they are the same size.

Other general strategies that students might use for dividing crazy cakes are the following:

■ To see or to show that two parts of a shape are congruent (the same shape), students may cut out the pieces and flip, turn, and slide them until they are exactly on top of one another, as in this division of example D.

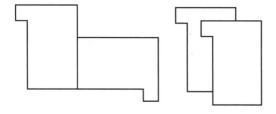

■ When a shape is not symmetrical, it is useful to cut off and move part of the shape to make the whole figure symmetrical before dividing the shape in half (this could have been done in example D). This is commonly referred to as "cut and paste," shown below for example H.

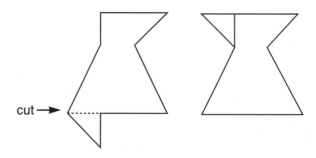

■ A more unusual method is to fold or cut and paste noncongruent halves so they equal the same shape, as in example B.

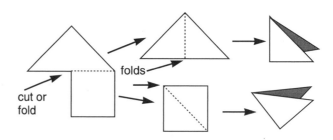

How Do You Know It's Half?

Dividing crazy cakes in half presents a good opportunity for students to work with area without using any numbers. It is an important basis for the rest of the unit, in which students work with fractional concepts by dividing areas into equivalent pieces. Being able to visualize how two pieces might have the same area even though they look different is an important part of what students do in the following sessions.

Does anyone have another way to "cut" cake A in half?

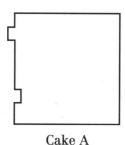

Cake A

Jesse: I have another way. [*Draws horizontal line with tab up at right-hand end.*]

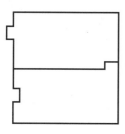

Jesse's Cake A

Nhat: It's backwards. That tab should go down.

Jesse: I did it that way to take away a piece from the top one that's the same as the extra piece.

Nhat: But now the top piece will have one more little piece.

Jesse: [He *cuts out the pieces to show Nhat how it works. He cuts off the tabs and puts them in the indentations.*] There's one tab there and one tab there. And they both have the same amount.

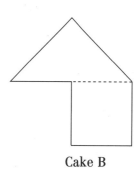

Cake B

I see that both Kumiko and Sarah have cut cake B by separating the triangle from the square. Can you explain to us how you know that the triangle and the square are equal pieces?

Kumiko: Rikki said before it looked like a rocket and all it needed was a top, so that gave me an idea. I put the square on top of the triangle. Then I cut off the extra pieces [*marked* a] and put them in here [*marked* b].

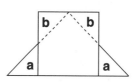

Kumiko's Cake B

Sarah, what did you do with cake B?

Sarah: I cut this part off [*the triangle marked* a] and moved it up to the top [*the triangular space marked* b].

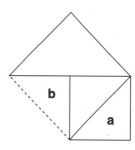

Sarah's Cake B

Halves, Fourths, and Eighths with Geoboards

Materials

- Geoboards with rubber bands (1 per pair)
- Stick-on notes (several per student)
- Transparencies of Student Sheet 2 (3 copies)
- Student Sheet 2 (2–3 per student)
- Student Sheet 3 (1 per student, optional)
- Student Sheet 4 (2 per student)
- Student Sheet 5 (1 per student, homework)
- Scissors (1 per pair)
- Crayons or markers
- Family letter (1 per student)
- Overhead projector

What Happens

Students divide a specified area (the square of a geoboard) into halves, fourths, and eighths. Students discuss their solutions and compare various-shaped fourths to show they are the same size. They write justifications for designs partitioned in fourths. Their work focuses on:

- exploring the relationships among halves, fourths, and eighths
- understanding that equal parts of a whole must be exactly equal in size
- understanding that equal parts of a whole do not need to be congruent
- justifying their division of area into equal parts

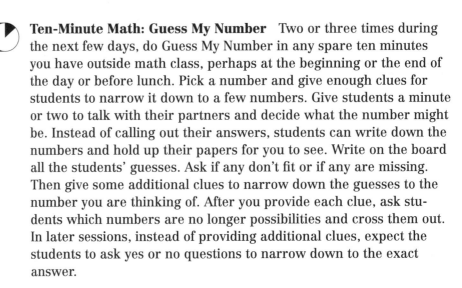

Ten-Minute Math: Guess My Number Two or three times during the next few days, do Guess My Number in any spare ten minutes you have outside math class, perhaps at the beginning or the end of the day or before lunch. Pick a number and give enough clues for students to narrow it down to a few numbers. Give students a minute or two to talk with their partners and decide what the number might be. Instead of calling out their answers, students can write down the numbers and hold up their papers for you to see. Write on the board all the students' guesses. Ask if any don't fit or if any are missing. Then give some additional clues to narrow down the guesses to the number you are thinking of. After you provide each clue, ask students which numbers are no longer possibilities and cross them out. In later sessions, instead of providing additional clues, expect the students to ask yes or no questions to narrow down to the exact answer.

You might start with a square number and use the geoboard to illustrate it. **I am thinking of a square number less than 100. It is an odd number. Remember, square numbers are numbers of objects that can be arranged in a square, like the 16 on the geoboard.** (Draw on the board the 4-by-4 square partitioned into 16 small squares and label length and width with 4 and the area inside as 16. Point out that square numbers are also answers when you multiply a number by itself, in this case 4×4.) Ask students what other squares can be made on the geoboard (1×1, 2×2, 3×3). Write their areas as a number series for students to continue: 1, 4, 9, 16, . . .

The square number I am thinking of is an odd number. What number could I be thinking of? Good guesses are 1, 9, 25, 49, and 81. Pick one of these as your answer and give information to narrow it down, such as for 25: **It is one-fourth of a hundred.** Or for 49: **It is a little less than half a hundred.**

In order to prepare students for the 4-by-6 rectangle they partition later in this investigation, use 24 as one of your numbers to guess. Say something like: **I am thinking of a number less than 40 that has more than 5 factors. What are all the numbers it could be?** Good guesses would include 12, 20, 24, 28, 30, 32, and 36. Suggest students narrow down the answer by asking you more about the factors. (The only odd factors are 1 and 3; 5, 7, and 9 are not factors. It is a multiple of 8.)

For full directions and variations of Guess My Number, see p. 55.

Halves on the Geoboard and Dot Paper

Introducing Geoboards Pass out the geoboards, one to each pair of students. If your students are using geoboards for the first time, give them some time to explore making shapes before they begin the work on fractions. Most students find geoboards intrinsically interesting and will want just to "mess around" before proceeding on to the structured activities in the unit. (You will probably want to come to an agreement with students about keeping the rubber bands out of the air and on the boards!)

After sufficient exploration time, model for students some ways to use the geoboard to investigate area and fractions. First, show students on the geoboard the whole square they will be dividing into fractional parts. Place a large rubber band around all the outside pins.

This is the largest square you can make on a geoboard. This is the square you will be dividing into fractions when you work with geoboards.

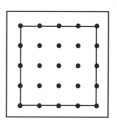

Wrap a rubber band around one of the small squares on the geoboard.

Suppose we count this small square as 1. How many of these small squares are there in the whole geoboard? We're finding its area.

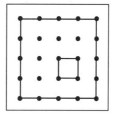

Place a rubber band from corner to
diagonal corner on the board.

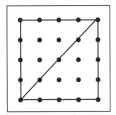

**How large is each of the triangles I made by putting this rubber band on
the geoboard?**

Students are likely to recognize that each piece is a half (as in the crazy
cakes activity), and some will know that it therefore has eight square units.
Ask them how they know. Point to one of the triangles:

**What is the area of this triangle—that is,
how many of the little squares are in it?**

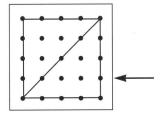

It is important in the discussion about these shapes that students identify
two different ways of knowing that there are 8 squares. Some students will
count the area in one triangle, combining the half-unit triangles along the
rubber band into squares. Students also should realize logically that there
must be 8 small squares on each side of the diagonal because the whole
square is 16 small squares, the diagonal divides the square into halves, and
half of 16 is 8. Students will need to use both counting unit squares and
thinking about relationships in the whole in the next several sessions.

Introducing Dot Paper Pass out Student Sheet 2, Dot-Paper Squares.
Note that the squares are similar to the large squares on the geoboards.
Draw a few examples of these dot-paper squares on the chalkboard or use
an overhead transparency of Student Sheet 2. Ask students what different
ways they could divide this square in half. Students will probably first come
up with using one horizontal, vertical, or diagonal cut as shown:

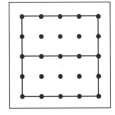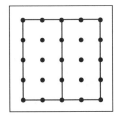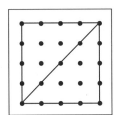

If students do not come up with a way to divide the square in half in a more unusual way, ask if a student can suggest an example of one:

These solutions use straight lines to divide the square in half. Can anyone show a way to divide the geoboard into two equal parts using something other than one straight line?

Typically, very little prompting is needed to get students making more interesting halves, and by working together they will get even more ideas. You can draw one of the following to provide an example of using something other than straight lines. The two figures at the right also show that the halves do not need to be the same shape.

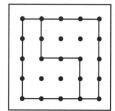 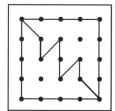 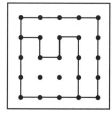 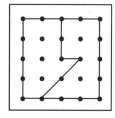

For each unusual idea offered by your students, ask them how they know that the two parts are equal in area. When the parts are congruent, encourage explanations that don't involve counting, such as turning one half upside down to show that it is just the same as the other half.

Finding Halves of the Large Squares   Using geoboards and recording their solutions on the dot-paper squares (Student Sheet 2), students work in pairs to create as many different ways as they can of dividing the area of the large geoboard square in half. Each student should fill out an individual student sheet.

There are a few rules about making halves that will hold for similar activities in the rest of this unit:

■ Each half must be contiguous—that is, it can't have two or more disconnected pieces.

■ Each solution must use all the area of the figure. It is against the rules to throw away some of the area and divide what remains into fractional parts.

Share these rules with your students at the beginning of the activity and keep them in mind as you walk around observing their work.

Observing the Students   As you circulate among the small groups, observe the strategies students are using, and check to make sure they are reasoning about area (as opposed to pins). Use the following questions to guide your observations:

■ How do students divide squares in half? Are they reasoning about the *area* of the squares?

Some students make the mistake of making halves that evenly split the number of *pins* instead of the area. This method often does not result in parts with equal areas. Notice that one of the halves illustrated has three dots inside, some have two, some have one, and one has no dots inside. Suggest to students who are counting pins to think about the crazy cakes examples, where they looked at the whole shape.

Suppose this geoboard was a cake that you wanted to share with a friend. Would it be fair for you to get this piece (point to one of the pieces) and for your friend to get the other piece? How can you prove whether or not it's fair?

Or, you might ask another student to show how to look at the area of the figure instead.

- What do students' halves look like? Do they recognize that equal parts of a whole must be equal in area? Do they realize that equal pieces are not necessarily congruent?
- How do students prove that their squares are divided in half? Do they cut and paste visually? Do they reason with the small unit squares? Do they use knowledge of the whole and parts to find out what's left? Do they have multiple strategies for proving equivalence of areas?

Once students have had a chance to generate some different halves, ask several students to share with the class how their halves are equal in area. You might select one or two students whose halves resulted in shapes that look different. If no one has a shape with parts that are not congruent, then put one on the overhead or chalkboard and challenge the class to prove or disprove that the shape is cut in half. You might challenge pairs of students who seem ready for it to then find halves that do not have the same shape.

If you think your students should have more practice with halves before moving on, ask them to make a page of their favorite halves. Then have them exchange papers to check each other's work.

Activity

Fourths and Eighths

As students are ready to go on to find fourths and eighths, review with them the meaning of *fourths* and *eighths* (for example, one-fourth is "one of four equal parts of the whole"). Students often know the word *fourths*, especially as it fits in the series: thirds, fourths, fifths, sixths, and so on. The fact that the word *quarter* is, in some contexts, a synonym for *fourth* may be less familiar to them.

The last couple of days you have been sharing cakes equally between two people, and using geoboard and dot paper to find halves. What if we shared the cake among four people instead of two? How much cake would each person get?

As students share their ideas, note whether anyone uses "one-fourth" or "one quarter" in his or her discussion. If students do not mention these terms, introduce them now, and show students the notation. Then pose a similar question about eighths:

What if eight people wanted to share the cake equally. How much cake would each person get?

If students do not use the term "one-eighth" to describe such a portion, introduce it now and show the notation for it.

Why do you think that *quarter* might mean the same thing as *fourth*?

Students create a number of examples of both fourths and eighths using Student Sheet 2. If students combine solutions for these two fractions on the same page, ask them to label each square as "fourths" or "eighths." As you circulate among the students, ask them to justify how they know that their division has produced fourths (or eighths):

Is this a "fair" division into fourths (or eighths)? How do you know for sure?

Can you use any of your patterns for fourths to help you create more eighths?

Once students have made some interesting fourths, suggest they find solutions combining different fourths in the same square. Challenge them to find a way to make four fourths in the same square, all different in shape.

See the **Teacher Note**, Students' Work on Fourths and Eighths (p. 16), for some examples.

Many students at this point will have stopped using the geoboard to find divisions of the square and will just draw directly on the grid-paper squares. They will need to work without the geoboard to continue this work at home. At any point in the exploration, however, geoboards are still useful for discussions among students or between you and the students, since the rubber bands can be moved easily to experiment with different configurations.

When students have had some experience dividing squares into fourths and eighths, ask them about quarters and fourths:

Why do you think that *quarter* might mean the same as *fourth*? Why do people say, "We have a quarter of a mile to go" or "It's a quarter after four."

Students are more likely to remember the correspondence between *fourth* and *quarter* if they make the connection between *quarter* as a fraction and *quarter* as a coin that is worth one fourth of a dollar.

You may wish to demonstrate the correspondence between *quarter* and *fourth* on a circular clock by showing how the area swept by the minute hand in a quarter of an hour is one-fourth the area of the face of the clock.

At the end of Session 2, suggest that students continue their work for homework. Pass out additional copies of Student Sheet 2 as needed (see p. 15 for more comments on homework).

A Page of Favorite Fourths

When students have done a good deal of exploring how to make fourths and eighths, each student creates a page of his or her favorite ways of partitioning the square into fourths. (Since there are fewer options for the shape of individual eighths, partitioning into fourths presents a more interesting task for students.)

While students are working, take around a transparency of Student Sheet 2 to collect single fourths—in this situation, shapes with an area of four units—and to draw a different one on each of the dot squares. Draw the four-unit square and a strip of four on the first two squares and then pick out a variety of others from among the students' favorite fourths. Label each of the shapes with a letter for identification in discussion. If you don't have access to an overhead projector, make a sheet of shapes and copy it for students to look at. See the **Teacher Note**, Equal Fourths? (p. 17), for some examples of single fourths.

As students complete their pages of favorite fourths, they post them so others can look at them now or at any time before you bring the class together to discuss them. As students walk around the room looking at other students' work, suggest that they put stick-on notes with their names or initials on examples they have questions about.

Equal Fourths?

Bring the class together for students to discuss any of the favorite fourths other students found confusing and to compare fourths you collected on a transparency. This is a chance for students to be "teacher" and present their arguments using the overhead. If you do not have an overhead, students can put the designs on geoboards and hold them up for the class to view. Students using the overhead projector draw on a transparency copy of Student Sheet 2 any shapes they want to discuss.

First, the authors of any controversial partitionings into fourths can explain their thinking. Next, show the students the sheet of fourths you prepared and challenge them to prove the fourths are all the same size.

These are all fourths I copied from your sheets. They are all fourths of the whole geoboard square, so they must all be the same size. Think how

you might prove they are the same size without using any numbers except half. How might you cut and paste this figure to show it is the same size as the strips or the squares that we know are fourths?

Invite students to pick one and go up to the front of the room to explain that it must be a fourth because it is the same as another one already proven. Encourage students to question one another until they see it and encourage them to show different ways to compare a single figure. See the **Teacher Note**, Equal Fourths? (p. 17) for some sample explanations.

Activity

Teacher Checkpoint

Writing Proofs for Fractional Parts

After these two sessions, provide students with designs for fractional parts that they must prove in writing. You can choose designs yourself or use those on Student Sheet 3, Proving Fractional Parts. If you make up your own, choose designs in which the parts are not all the same shape, as in example 3, to see if your students think parts that are not congruent can still have equal areas. Students can explain the fractional parts using words and/or diagrams. Focus on students' ability to describe and/or diagram why and how the parts are equal in area.

Use the following questions to guide your observations of students' work on this activity:

- Are students convinced that the fractional parts are equal? How do they prove it? Do they focus on the area instead of the pins? Do they count squares or parts of squares correctly? Do they use cut-and-paste arguments appropriately? ("If I cut off part of this shape and paste it on over here, then they would be exactly the same shape.")
- How do students use words and/or diagrams to prove that fractional parts are the same? Are their proofs convincing? Can you follow students' reasoning?

See the **Teacher Note**, Students Write About Fractions (p. 18), for some samples of the sorts of arguments and diagrams your students might use in proving the equality of fractional parts.

Activity

Making a Fourths Quilt

Give each student two copies of Student Sheet 4, Squares for a Quilt of Fourths, one for doing a draft version and one for doing a final version of a quilt pattern. Students divide each of the small squares into fourths in a different way. They use their favorite fourths or make up new ways of partitioning into fourths. They color each square's fourths using the same four colors. It is easier for students to do this if they color each square right after they divide it into four parts. Students may take these home to finish. The quilts can be cut out from the student sheet and displayed along the top edge of a wall to form a frieze.

Sessions 2, 3, and 4 Follow-Up

🏠 **Homework**

Dot-Paper Squares After Session 2, send home the family letter or *Investigations* at Home. Students will also need Student Sheet 2, Dot-Paper Squares. For homework, students should finish dividing the squares into fourths and eighths or work on their page of favorite fourths, depending on how far they have progressed in class.

Dividing into Fourths After Session 3, students continue working at home on favorite fourths.

A Favorite Fourth After Session 4, students choose one of their favorite fourths, one they think is the most interesting, and record it on Student Sheet 5, A Favorite Fourth. For homework, students write about how they would prove that each part is one-fourth and that all four parts are equal.

Teacher Note ▷ *Students' Work on Fourths and Eighths*

Students are likely to see quickly some of the common ways of dividing a square into fourths and then into eighths, but they will have to think harder about more irregular ways. Here are some:

Rashaida's:
Some different

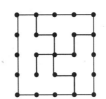

Luisa's :
All congruent

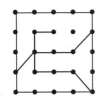

B.J.'s: All different

One interesting way to generate fourths is to start with a simple division into fourths, such as example A, and to cut a small piece from each fourth to add to the next fourth, as in example B. As long as you do the same thing to all four

fourths, the resulting figure will also be divided into equal fourths. This is a fairly sophisticated argument for students to understand, but if you show them an example, they are likely to use it to generate more examples.

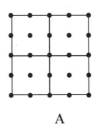

A   B

When working with eighths, students will likely first come up with a picture like Kim's, below. Others may then modify it to something like Jesse's. More unusual eighths, like Qi Sun's, may emerge more slowly, as these eighths require a deeper understanding.

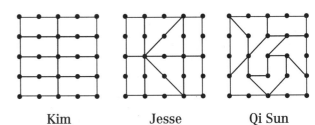

Kim   Jesse   Qi Sun

Equal Fourths?

tion and *quarter* as a coin that is worth one fourth of a dollar.

You may wish to demonstrate the correspon-

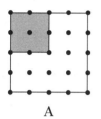 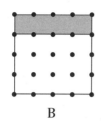

A   B

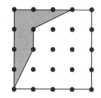 

dence between *quarter* and *fourth* on a circular clock by showing how the area swept by the

minute hand in a quarter of an hour is one-fourth the area of the face of the clock.

At the end of Session 2, suggest that students continue their work for homework. Pass out additional copies of Student Sheet 2 as needed (see
p. 15 for more comments on homework).

When students have done a good deal of exploring how to make fourths and eighths, each student creates a page of his or her favorite ways of partitioning the square into fourths. (Since there are fewer options for the shape of individual eighths, partitioning into fourths presents a more interesting task for students.)

While students are working, take around a transparency of Student Sheet 2 to collect single fourths—in this situation, shapes with an area of four units—and to draw a different one on each of the dot squares. Draw the four-unit square and a strip of four on the first two squares and then pick out a variety of others from among the students' favorite fourths. Label each of the shapes with a letter for identification in discussion. If you don't have access to an overhead projector, make a sheet of shapes and copy it for students to look at. See the **Teacher Note**, Equal Fourths? (p. 17), for some examples of single fourths.

As students complete their pages of favorite fourths, they post them so others can look at them now or at any time before you bring the class together to discuss them. As students walk around the room looking at other students' work, suggest that they put stick-on notes with their names or initials on

examples they have questions about.

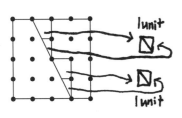

Bring the class together for students to discuss any of the favorite fourths other students found confusing and to compare fourths you collected on a transparency. This is a chance for students to be "teacher" and present their arguments using the overhead. If you do not have an overhead, students can put the designs on geoboards and hold them up for the class to view. Students using the overhead projector draw on a transparency copy of Student Sheet 2 any shapes they want to discuss.

First, the authors of any controversial partitionings into

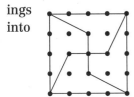

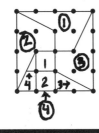

fourths can explain their thinking. Next, show the students the sheet of fourths you prepared and challenge them to prove the fourths are all the same size.

These are all fourths I copied from your sheets. They are all fourths of the whole geoboard square, so they must all be the same size.

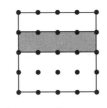 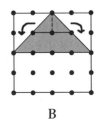

Think how A B

you might prove they are the same size without using any numbers except half. How might you cut and paste this figure to show it is the same size as the strips or the squares that we know are fourths?

Invite students to pick one and go up to the front of the room to explain that it must be a fourth because it is the same as another one already proven. Encourage students to question one another until they see it and encourage them to show different ways to compare a single figure. See the **Teacher Note**, Equal Fourths? (p. 17) for some sample explanations.

After these two sessions, provide students with designs for fractional parts that they must prove in writing. You can choose designs yourself or use those on Student Sheet 3, Proving Fractional Parts. If you make up your own, choose designs in which the parts are not all the same shape, as in example 3, to see if your students think parts that are not congruent can still have equal areas. Students can explain the fractional parts using words and/or diagrams. Focus on students' abil-

Combining Fractions in a Design

What Happens

Students construct ways of dividing a whole into a combination of halves, fourths, and eighths. They make drafts on small dot-paper squares, then copy a favorite onto a large square. After finishing this large square, students write equations that reflect the relationships their designs illustrate. Their work focuses on:

- exploring relationships among halves, fourths, and eighths
- writing equations that reflect pictures with halves, fourths, and eighths

Materials

- Scissors (1 per pair)
- Student Sheet 2 (1–2 per student)
- Student Sheet 6 (1–2 per student)
- Glue sticks (1 per pair)
- Crayons or markers
- Rulers (1 per pair)

Activity

Combining Halves, Fourths, and Eighths

Provide each student with a copy of Student Sheet 2, Dot-Paper Squares. In pairs or individually, students work on rough drafts of designs that include halves, fourths, and eighths. They will eventually transfer their favorite of these designs to a larger square on Student Sheet 6, Large Dot Square for Combining Fractions. You can introduce the task like this:

Many different designs will work to solve this next problem. The only rule is that you have to include halves, fourths, and eighths in the same dot-paper square.

You can use the examples you've already made for these fractions to give you ideas. Once you have designed a combination you especially like, you can put it on a large square.

A variety of strategies for dividing up the square will probably emerge. Many students will first determine the number of square units they need to include in each fractional part. Some others may create halves, then reason that a fourth is half of a half, and so on, without referring to units. Others will use examples of halves, fourths, and eighths they've already created and transfer these to a single dot square. Still others may decide to do some cutting or folding. Before they transfer their favorite design to large dot paper, they need to prove it to you.

Making Finished Drawings   Students transfer their favorite completed and proven designs to Student Sheet 6, the large dot-paper square. Encourage them to make their final designs as precise and clear as they can by using a straightedge to make their lines and by labeling each part of their designs with the appropriate fraction notations. Students can color in the parts of their combined-fraction designs with markers or crayons if they want to.

Students who finish this task before others can begin the next activity, Writing Fraction Relationships, or create additional finished drawings from other ideas they have worked out.

Writing Fraction Relationships

When students have completed a design of combined fractions, write on the chalkboard:

$$\frac{1}{8} \quad = \quad \text{half of a fourth}$$

$$\frac{1}{2} \quad = \quad \frac{2}{4}$$

Ask students to figure out how their squares can prove these relationships.

Can you prove these equations using your square? Can they be proven with all of your squares?

This is the first time in this unit that students will be considering fractions with numerators larger than one. Show students that a shorthand for writing $1/4 + 1/4$ is to write $2/4$.

Go on to other fractional relationships that can be found in the combined-fraction squares:

What are some other equations you can demonstrate with your square?

Collect a few examples.

What are some ways of making a whole that you can show with your square?

Collect examples of making one whole, such as:

$$1 = \frac{2}{8} + \frac{1}{2} + \frac{1}{4}$$

After the class discusses a few examples, students write facts about fractions they can demonstrate on their own square below their combined-fraction square. In addition to the types above, these may include strings of equivalents:

$$\frac{1}{2} = \frac{2}{4} = \frac{4}{8}$$

and equations that include addition on both sides of the equation:

$$\frac{1}{2} + \frac{1}{2} = \frac{2}{4} + \frac{4}{8}$$

As you circulate among students, challenge them to include equations of the various types shown above, though each student need not come up with every type. Ask students to show you that their equations work by using their square to demonstrate the relationships. You can post their finished squares with equations around the room.

Begin a class list of fraction equations and equivalents on poster paper that can be left up and added to as you go through the rest of this unit. You might make two separate lists: one for relationships among halves, fourths, and eighths and the second for relationships among thirds, sixths, twelfths, and halves.

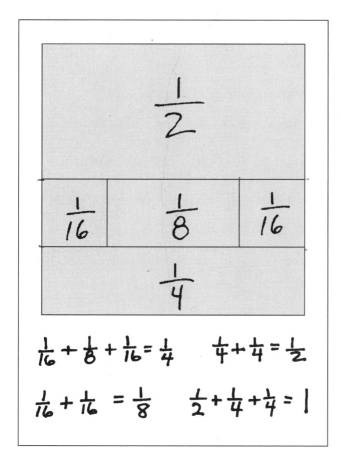

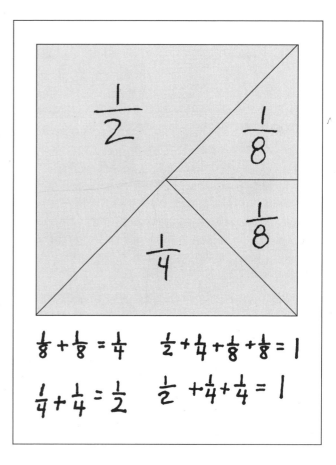

Session 5 Follow-Up

Large Dot Square for Combining Fractions   Students who have not finished at least one large square on Student Sheet 6 with corresponding equations can do so for homework. Those students who have already finished one sheet, including several equations, can choose another of the designs they worked out and complete another sheet.

 **Homework**

Parts of Rectangles: Thirds, Sixths, and Twelfths

What Happens

Sessions 1 and 2: Thirds, Sixths, and Twelfths
Students use a larger whole to explore size and equivalence relationships among fractions based on one-third. They divide dot-paper rectangles (as opposed to squares) into thirds, sixths, and, optionally, twelfths. They discuss that a fraction of these rectangles is larger than the same fraction of the squares with which they have been working. Each student makes a page of favorite sixths to keep.

Session 3: More Fraction Designs Students combine fractions based on one-third and fractions based on one-half in one design using a larger version of the dot-paper rectangle. They make a draft on a small version of the rectangle, transfer it to a large version, and write equations reflecting the relationships their design demonstrates.

Session 4: Working with 2/3, 3/4, 5/6, and 7/8
Student pairs create squares with specified frac-

tions of their area colored (two-thirds, three-fourths, five-sixths, and seven-eighths). The fraction of the square's area that is colored may be kept as one piece or broken up into several non-connected regions that together equal the specified amount. After finishing their own designs, students figure out how much of other students' designs are colored.

Mathematical Emphasis

- Knowing that equal fractions of different-sized wholes will be different in area
- Becoming familiar with relationships among thirds, sixths, and twelfths
- Using different combinations to make a whole
- Comparing fractions that have "one piece missing"
- Working with fractions that have numerators larger than one

What to Plan Ahead of Time

Materials

- Rulers: 1 per student pair (all sessions)
- Crayons or markers (all sessions)
- Small stick-on notes: several for each student (Sessions 1–2)
- Scissors: 1 per pair (Session 4, optional)
- Colored paper (Session 4, optional)
- Glue sticks: 1 per 3–4 students (Session 4, optional)
- Overhead projector, transparencies, and pens (Session 4)
- Geoboards: 1 per pair (Sessions 1–2)
- Calculators: 1 per pair (Ten-Minute Math)

Other Preparation

- Duplicate student sheets and teaching resources (located at the end of this unit) in the following quantities. If you have Student Activity Booklets, copy only the transparencies marked with an asterisk.

For Sessions 1–2

Student Sheet 7, A Dot-Paper Square and Rectangle (p. 67): 1 per pair and 1 overhead transparency*

Student Sheet 8, Dot-Paper Rectangles (p. 68): 5 per student and 1 for sessions 1–3

Student Sheet 9, Thirds and Sixths (p. 69): 1 per student (homework)

For Session 3

Student Sheet 10, Proving Thirds and Sixths (p. 70): 1 per student

Student Sheet 11, Large Dot Rectangle for Combining Fraction (p. 71): 3 per student (1 for homework)

For Session 4

Student Sheet 12, Blank Square (p. 72): 2 per student

Student Sheet 13, Agree or Disagree? (p. 74): 1 per student

How Much Is Colored?* (p. 75): 1 overhead transparency

Thirds, Sixths, and Twelfths

Materials

- Rulers (1 per pair)
- Crayons or markers
- Student Sheet 7 (1 per pair)
- Transparency of Student Sheet 7
- Student Sheet 8 (4 per student)
- Student Sheet 9 (1 per student, homework)
- Geoboard (1 for teacher demonstration)
- Calculators (1 per pair, Ten-Minute Math)
- Small stick-on notes (several per student)
- Overhead projector

What Happens

Students use a larger whole to explore size and equivalence relationships among fractions based on one-third. They divide dot-paper rectangles (as opposed to squares) into thirds, sixths, and, optionally, twelfths. They discuss that a fraction of these rectangles is larger than the same fraction of the squares with which they have been working. Each student makes a page of favorite sixths to keep. Their work focuses on:

- exploring the relationships among thirds, sixths, and twelfths
- understanding that the same fraction of different-sized wholes will be different in area
- being able to justify their division of rectangles into thirds, sixths, and twelfths

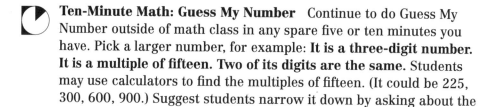 **Ten-Minute Math: Guess My Number** Continue to do Guess My Number outside of math class in any spare five or ten minutes you have. Pick a larger number, for example: **It is a three-digit number. It is a multiple of fifteen. Two of its digits are the same.** Students may use calculators to find the multiples of fifteen. (It could be 225, 300, 600, 900.) Suggest students narrow it down by asking about the digits in the number—for example, does it have a 3?

When students are comfortable with the activity, give them less information and expect them to narrow down the number by asking you questions to which you can answer yes or no. Limit the number of questions they can ask about the size of the number (Is it bigger than 500? Is it between 200 and 300?). Suggest that they ask you questions about its factors (Is it odd? Is it a multiple of ____?). For variations of Guess My Number, see p. 56.

Working with Thirds and Sixths

Put a transparency of Student Sheet 7, A Dot-Paper Square and Rectangle, on the overhead and pass out 1 copy of Student Sheet 7 to each pair of students. Also distribute one copy of Student Sheet 8 to each student.

Examining Fractions of Different Wholes Before you introduce thirds and sixths, your students need to consider the new dot paper they will be working with. The fact that the dot-paper rectangles on Student Sheet 8 have a different area from the dot-paper square on Student Sheet 7 can be confusing for your students. A potentially confusing fact, for example, is that half of the rectangle (12 small squares) is larger than half of the square (8 small squares). A third of the rectangle is the same area as half of the square—both are 8 small squares in area. In order to have students focus on the fact that *equal fractions of different-sized wholes are different,* display the transparency of Student Sheet 7 for all students to see.

Point to the dot-paper square as you review with students the total number of small squares in it. Compare it to the total number of small squares in the dot-paper rectangle on the transparency.

Pretend that each of these is a cake. You can choose one to share fairly with a friend. Which one would you choose? Why?

Students discuss this question in pairs or small groups before sharing their ideas with the whole class. Encourage students to reason about the size or area of the halves.

Do you think that half of the rectangle will have more or fewer small squares than half of the square? Why?

Then ask students to figure it out exactly. Draw a diagonal on the rectangle on the overhead and label it *Halves.*

How many squares are in half of this rectangle? How does half of the rectangle compare to half of the square?

Even after students have discussed the new whole, it is important that you listen for students still thinking that eight squares is equal to one-half, no matter what the whole. If this kind of thinking is widespread, reiterate the points above about the differences in area between the dot square and the dot rectangle.

Finding Thirds   Begin by asking students about a sharing situation involving three people.

We have been sharing things, like cake, among 2 people, 4 people, and 8 people—finding halves, fourths, and eighths. What if we shared a cake among 3 people instead of two? How much cake would each person get?

If anyone uses "one-third" as a way to describe this portion, ask that student to explain what "one-third" means. If students do not know about thirds, explain that they are three equal parts. If you want to share a cake equally among three people, you divide it into thirds.

Tell students that they will now be looking for thirds. Distribute Student Sheet 8, Dot-Paper Rectangles.

How can you divide one of the rectangles on Student Sheet 8 into thirds?

After each student has done this, have two or three present different solutions. You may choose to have students draw their solutions on either the board or the overhead. Ask the class:

How can we be sure each rectangle is divided into thirds?

How many small squares are in one-third of the rectangle? That many squares was what fraction of the square?

Students may find working with thirds difficult, even if they have been successful with halves, fourths, and eighths. Halves, fourths, and eighths are easier to understand because they can all be created by halving over and over (for example, a fourth is half of a half). Understanding thirds requires understanding a different way to divide a whole. Some students jump to the conclusion that thirds are three units, perhaps because fourths were four units in the square. Review the definition of *fourths* as four equal parts that take up the whole area and ask students what the definition of *thirds* must be. They need to understand that thirds (and sixths) of one whole, like fourths, must be exactly equal in area. They may not look the same, but they must have the same number of square units.

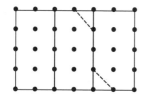

Generating Examples Students now work in pairs to create a page of thirds and a page of sixths. Once they have made simple thirds, they can make new thirds. As they may have done with fourths, some students might take a small piece from one third and add it to another third, thus making interesting thirds. Some students will make sixths by halving their thirds. For a strategy a student invented, see the **Teacher Note**, A Strategy for Finding Interesting Thirds (p. 28).

Students can work on their own if they choose, but they must verify their solutions with another student. Circulate among students and explore how they are thinking about this activity. They should be able to justify their responses as before. Challenge students to come up with "unusual" thirds and thirds that don't all have the same shape, as they did before with halves and fourths. Expect that some students will argue by counting units of area, while others will "see" the equivalence between two areas. As with partitioning areas of squares, be sure students count area, not dots.

You can present the task of dividing the rectangle into *sixths* at the same time as the introduction of thirds, or you may visit students as they work on thirds and suggest they go on to sixths when you think they've done sufficient work on thirds. In either case, encourage students to use their prior solutions for halves and thirds to help them think of more possibilities for sixths. Some students may also want to investigate twelfths.

A Page of Favorite Thirds and Sixths

Once students have finished making thirds and sixths in their pairs, they make final copies of their favorite solutions for thirds and sixths, with both fractions on one page or a page of each. It is fine if pairs of students who have collaborated use similar examples to make their individual pages. The important criterion is that students need to be confident the solutions they choose in fact show sixths accurately and that they can prove this to another person.

As with favorite fourths, you might post students' pages of favorites so they can put stick-on notes on ones they don't understand. Or you can collect from students a variety of partitionings into thirds and sixths on an overhead transparency for students to discuss.

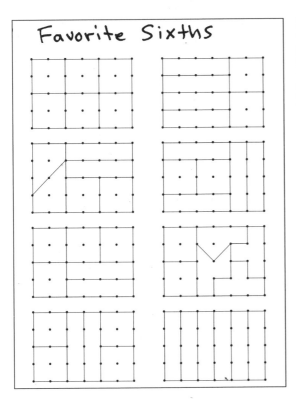

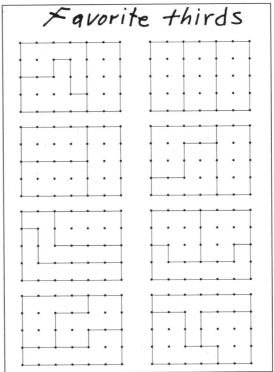

Sessions 1 and 2 Follow-Up

Dot-Paper Rectangles   After Session 1, students may complete their pages of thirds or sixths or make a page of favorites.

Thirds and Sixths   After Session 2, give each student a copy of Student Sheet 9, Thirds and Sixths. Students divide one rectangle into thirds and one into sixths and explain how they know each rectangle is divided into equal parts.

A Strategy for Finding Interesting Thirds

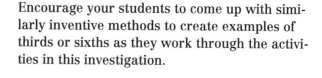

While making thirds and sixths may be a difficult task, it leads students to construct firmer ideas about the relationships among sixths and thirds and about the nature of fractional parts. During this work, listen for interesting discoveries or strategies that students invent. You may want to share these with the whole class. For example, one student who was working on thirds started with this pattern:

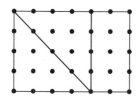

He then invented the following strategy: "If you cover up the rectangle on the (right) side, then you have the squares, like we used before, so just do halves. You can use all your old halves ways, then uncover the other rectangle and you have thirds!"

Encourage your students to come up with similarly inventive methods to create examples of thirds or sixths as they work through the activities in this investigation.

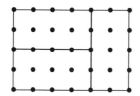

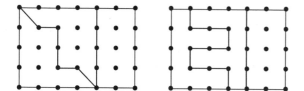

More Fraction Designs

What Happens

Students combine fractions based on one-third and fractions based on one-half in one design using a larger version of the dot-paper rectangle. They make a draft on a small version of the rectangle, transfer it to a large version, and write equations reflecting the relationships their design demonstrates. Their work focuses on:

- visualizing the relationships among 1/2, 1/3, 1/4, 1/6, 1/8, and 1/12
- writing equations that reflect the relationships among these fractions

Materials

- Rulers (1 per pair)
- Crayons or markers
- Student Sheet 8 (1 per student)
- Student Sheet 10 (1 per student)
- Student Sheet 11 (3 per student)

Activity

After students have had several experiences with thirds and sixths, have them do the assessment on Student Sheet 10, Proving Thirds and Sixths:

Assessment

Proving Thirds and Sixths

1. Is this rectangle divided into thirds? Explain your answer.

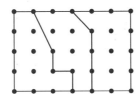

2a. Is this rectangle divided into sixths? Explain your answer.

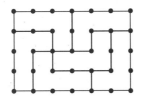

2b. Color one-third of the rectangle. Explain how you know it is one-third.

3. Some students say 1/6 is larger than 1/4 because 6 is larger than 4. What do you think? Explain.

See the **Teacher Note,** Assessment: Proving Thirds and Sixths (p. 32), for some things to consider when evaluating students' responses.

Activity

Making a Combined Design

Each student first works out a design that includes many different fractions (1/2, 1/3, 1/4, 1/6, 1/8, 1/12) on a regular dot rectangle (Student Sheet 8). Encourage students to take the time to experiment and verify that their solutions accurately show each fraction. They then transfer their finished designs to the large rectangle (Student Sheet 11), labeling each part with its fraction and coloring the design, if desired. Students are likely to count squares to determine the different fractions.

As with the earlier combining-fractions activity, students then write all the equations they can find that are demonstrated by their design. You might want to post these combined fractions designs. Finally, students come together to add fraction equations to the large class list and discuss how their drawings illustrate these equations.

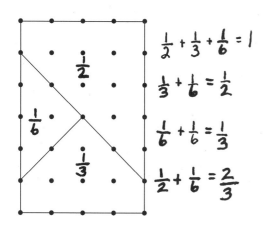

$$\frac{1}{2} + \frac{1}{3} + \frac{1}{6} = 1$$

$$\frac{1}{3} + \frac{1}{6} = \frac{1}{2}$$

$$\frac{1}{6} + \frac{1}{6} = \frac{1}{3}$$

$$\frac{1}{2} + \frac{1}{6} = \frac{2}{3}$$

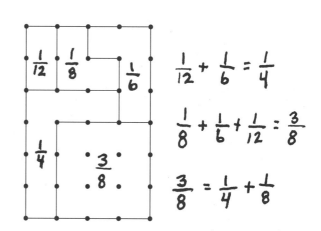

$$\frac{1}{12} + \frac{1}{6} = \frac{1}{4}$$

$$\frac{1}{8} + \frac{1}{6} + \frac{1}{12} = \frac{3}{8}$$

$$\frac{3}{8} = \frac{1}{4} + \frac{1}{8}$$

Session 3 Follow-Up

Large Dot Rectangle for Combining Fractions   Students can finish their large rectangles for homework if they have not already finished them in class. Those who have finished can create another. Challenge them to get as many fractions as possible into the rectangle (perhaps 3/8, 1/12, 1/4, 1/6, and 1/8). Give students another copy of Student Sheet 11 to make a second design and remind them to take their copies of Student Sheet 8 home with them so they can use designs they have already worked out.

 **Homework**

Writing Equations Equal to 1   Now that students have worked with a variety of fractions, they can add many more equations to their list of fraction relationships. Challenge them to find as many ways as they can to equal one whole.

 **Extensions**

Making Fractional Flags   Using plain paper, grid paper, or the large dot-paper rectangle (Student Sheet 11), students design flags with different fractions colored different colors. For example, flags may be one-third green, one-sixth yellow, and one-half red. The fractional parts in this case do not have to be contiguous; fractional parts are determined only by their color. Students write about the fractional color parts in their flags.

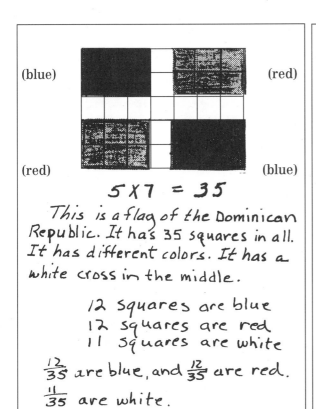

(blue) (red) (red) (blue)

$5 \times 7 = 35$

This is a flag of the Dominican Republic. It has 35 squares in all. It has different colors. It has a white cross in the middle.

12 squares are blue
12 squares are red
11 squares are white

$\frac{12}{35}$ are blue, and $\frac{12}{35}$ are red.
$\frac{11}{35}$ are white.

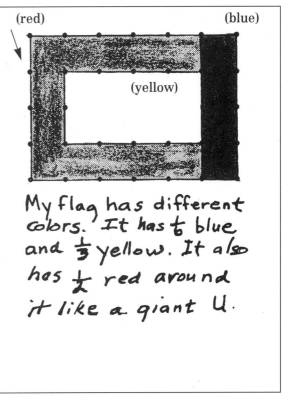

(red)   (blue)

(yellow)

My flag has different colors. It has $\frac{1}{6}$ blue and $\frac{1}{3}$ yellow. It also has $\frac{1}{2}$ red around it like a giant U.

Use this assessment to take a look at students' facility in dealing with simple fractions in terms of area, including:

■ Do they know that equal parts of a whole must be equal in area but not necessarily congruent?

■ Do they have multiple strategies for proving the equivalence of areas (visually cut and paste, reason with small unit squares, use knowledge of the whole and parts to find out what's left, and so on)?

■ Do they see and use relationships among related fractions, such as 1/3 and 1/6?

■ Do they know that the fraction depends on the number of equal parts rather than the number of units in each part (for example, one-third is one of three equal parts, not necessarily a part with three units of area)?

When evaluating students' responses to Student Sheet 10, consider their understanding of fractions and also their ability to compare areas visually.

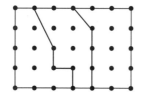

Problem 1

Problem 1 This student made a clear explanation based on counting units:

No, because section 3 has 8½ boxes and section 2 has 7½. That leaves section 1. I knew before I counted it that these were not thirds because section 2 and section 3 are not equal.

This student compares a piece with a mental image of a regular third made by partitioning with two vertical cuts:

No, because the last part is a third with an extra half piece without giving it back.

This student dealt with area as a whole without counting units at all:

No, because I traced them and cut them out and measured.

Problem 2a

Problem 2a Some students will count the units in each piece without noticing that the pieces are congruent. This student comes to a correct conclusion:

Yes, because every section has four boxes.

Note: If some students count and conclude that because there are four units, these are fourths, they need help understanding basic ideas about fractions.

Others will see the areas as wholes:

Yes, because they are all even spaces and there are six of them.

Yes, because if you piece it apart the Ls are the same size.

Problem 2b This question is about equivalence. Notice whether students color in two of the sixths already drawn, showing that they know two-sixths is equivalent to one third or whether they count out eight squares to make one-third without considering the relationship to sixths.

Problem 3 Look for the general idea that more pieces result in smaller pieces:

I think 1/4 is larger because the more pieces you cut a pie into, the smaller the piece is.

Here is an incomplete answer that does not articulate knowledge of this general idea:

1/4 is larger than 1/6 because 1/4 is a quarter.

Working with $^2/_3$, $^3/_4$, $^5/_6$, and $^7/_8$

What Happens

Student pairs create squares with specified fractions of their area colored (two-thirds, three-fourths, five-sixths, and seven-eighths). The fraction of the square's area that is colored may be kept as one piece or broken up into several nonconnected regions that together equal the specified amount. After finishing their own design, students figure out how much of other students' designs are colored. Their work focuses on:

■ using measurement to divide up a square into fractional parts

■ comparing fractions that have "one piece missing"

■ working with fractions that have a numerator larger than 1

Materials

■ Rulers (1 per pair)

■ Crayons or markers

■ Colored paper (optional)

■ Student Sheet 12 (2 per student)

■ Student Sheet 13 (1 per student)

■ Transparency of How Much Is Colored?

■ Scissors (1 per pair, optional)

■ Glue stick (1 per pair, optional)

■ Overhead projector

Activity

Begin the activity with examples to convey the idea to students. Display the transparency (or show a copy) of How Much Is Colored? (p. 75), which shows $^3/_4$ of the square colored, and ask:

How much of this square is colored? How much is not colored?

Ask students to explain how they know what fraction of the square is colored. If a student says "Half and a quarter is colored," write this answer on the board and ask what fraction of the total area of the square that would be altogether.

Repeat the process with the transparency of How Much Is Colored? (p. 76), which shows $^5/_6$ or $^{10}/_{12}$ of the square colored. If students count the pieces they will call it ten-twelfths. If they think of sliding the third piece in the bottom layer to the right, they will be able to see that it is also five-sixths.

Making Colored Squares

Tell students they are to make some of these colored squares. Each student pair should complete four different squares. List the fractions for the four squares on the board:

$\frac{3}{4}$ colored and $\frac{1}{4}$ uncolored

$\frac{2}{3}$ colored and $\frac{1}{3}$ uncolored

$\frac{5}{6}$ colored and $\frac{1}{6}$ uncolored

$\frac{7}{8}$ colored and $\frac{1}{8}$ uncolored

You do not have to make the part you color all one piece. For example, you can use six-eighths to show three-fourths colored, as in the example I showed you.

Encourage students to work together to plan the thirds or sixths colored examples, which are more difficult.

Making the Squares   Students work on copies of Student Sheet 12. The sides of the squares are premarked in useful intervals to facilitate easier division of the area of the square: page 1 is in sixths (useful for thirds and sixths), and page 2 is in eighths (useful for fourths and eighths). Let students decide for themselves which square to use. They can ignore the marking if they choose.

Experimentation in pencil that can be erased is to be encouraged here.

Use a pencil to plan your designs. Before you use color on your design, you need to be able to prove to your partner that your design will have the correct fraction of the square colored. Once you have sketched a design in pencil and proven that it works with your partner, you can use crayons or markers to color it. You may cut out colored paper to color it, if you want to.

Visit groups of students as they work to see how they are conceptualizing the task. Ask students who feel they have completed a design to prove to you that they have in fact shaded in the appropriate fraction of the square. While students don't need to label the parts of their squares with fraction symbols, they should be able to tell you what fractions are represented by the various regions.

Students write the fraction colored for each design on the back of their completed squares and their names on the front.

Comparing Squares Once students have completed their squares, they get together in groups of four (not with their partners). They exchange their designs so each is holding two designs that are not his or her own. Working as a group but with the author silent, they decide what fraction of each square is colored.

Make a large area available, perhaps on the chalkboard, for displaying the squares in groups. Put four headings for students to tape the squares under:

three-fourths $\frac{3}{4}$ two-thirds $\frac{2}{3}$ five-sixths $\frac{5}{6}$ seven-eighths $\frac{7}{8}$

Students place their squares under the heading they think fits.

Teacher Checkpoint

Agree or Disagree?

Ask students to look at the displays of the different colored squares from the previous activity, and then hand out Student Sheet 13, Agree or Disagree?, for them to respond to questions about the fractions.

Use the following questions to guide your observations of students' reasoning and their work:

■ How do students compare fractions with one piece missing? Do they understand that the size of the piece that is missing is different? Do they see that the more pieces you cut the whole into, the smaller the pieces? Or do they think that $3/8$ is bigger than $3/4$ because 8 is bigger than 4? See the **Teacher Note,** Accurate Drawings or Accurate Knowledge? (p. 37).

■ How do students interpret fractions with numerators larger than 1? How do they approximate four-fifths of a rectangle? Are students able to generate other fractions that are similar in size to $4/5$? What strategies do they use to do so?

■ How do students interpret and represent a fraction with a numerator larger than the denominator? How do they compare $3/2$ to $2/3$?

When students are finished, take time to discuss the problems and their answers. You may need to introduce the ideas of mixed numbers and fractions with numerator larger than denominator. In the next investigation, students will work on recognizing and comparing a variety of fractions and mixed numbers.

❖ **Tip for the Linguistically Diverse Classroom** Read aloud each problem on Student Sheet 13. After students with limited English proficiency have answered each question, have them provide their explanations with pictures only.

Session 4 Follow-Up

Writing About a Colored-Square Design   Students pick one of their col-ored-square designs and in the space beneath write about how they created it and how they know what fraction of it is colored. This can be started in class when they have finished Student Sheet 13.

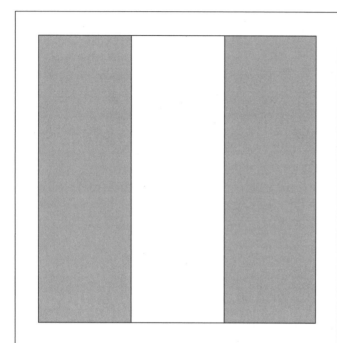

$\frac{2}{3}$ shaded. 3 strips make a whole. 2 strips make $\frac{2}{3}$.

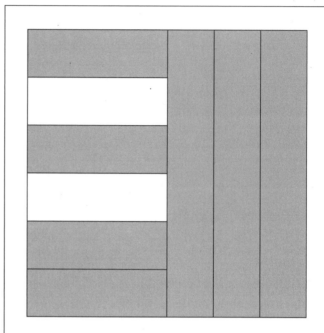

$\frac{5}{6}$ covered. I cut it into 6^{ths} and I used 5.

❖ **Tip for the Linguistically Diverse Classroom**   Offer limited English proficient students the option of writing in their native languages to explain how they created their designs. If students have not yet acquired this skill, have them show how they figured out their answer by using numbers and a drawing.

Students' Problems with Skip Counting

Student Sheet 13, Agree or Disagree?, is similar to an assessment, but because these fractions are just introduced in this session, we think you should simply consider it a checkpoint. It is an opportunity for you to see if students recognize that the fractions with different pieces missing are not all the same size and if they can interpret fractions with numerators larger than 1 and fractions with numerators larger than their denominators. Many students will base their comparisons on drawings. It is crucial that the wholes they draw be the same size.

Here one student, Nhat, kept the wholes the same size. He notes that the one-sixth space left is smaller than one-fourth space left, so five-sixths is larger than three-fourths.

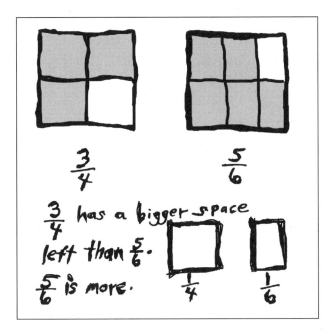

Another student, Sarah, makes each sixth and each fourth the same size so the wholes are different. She then, like Nhat, makes her decision based on the piece missing in her drawings and incorrectly concludes that 3/4 and 5/6 are the same size.

Sometimes students use drawings to solve problems, but often they decide on their answer first and then set about making an illustration that shows it. Look carefully at your students' drawings to see what they show you about what the students believe. Often messier drawings are correct while neater drawings illustrate confusions.

Ordering Fractions

What Happens

Sessions 1 and 2: Making Fraction Cards
Each group of four students makes a deck of 60 fraction cards on which they create visual representations of fractions, including fractions greater than 1. Collaboratively, they make a class deck that they will use to create two ordered fraction clotheslines. The class learns to play the game Fraction Fish to practice finding equivalent fractions.

Session 3: Ordering Fractions with Respect to Landmarks Groups of students sort their decks of fraction cards with respect to the landmarks 0, 1/2, 1, and 2. They discuss discrepancies between groups' sortings and decide as a class which sorting is correct.

Sessions 4 and 5: Making a Fraction Number Line Working in small groups, the class puts together two fraction number lines, each of which contains half of the fraction cards in the class deck, by hanging the cards in order from a long clothesline. In parallel, students play Capture Fractions (a game in which the larger fraction wins each round) with the decks of fraction cards they have made.

Mathematical Emphasis

Developing a variety of ways to compare fractions, including:

- Comparing any fraction to the landmarks 0, 1/2, 1, and 2

- Using both numerical reasoning and area to order fractions (for example, $4/9$ is smaller than $1/2$ because $2 \times 4/9 = 8/9$, which is less than 1)

- Using the size of the numerator to compare fractions that have the same denominator (for example, $2/4$ is less than $3/4$)

- Using the size of the denominator to compare fractions with the same numerator (for example, $2/3$ is larger than $2/4$ because thirds are larger than fourths)

- Comparing fractions greater than 1 with fractions less than or equal to 1 (for example, $4/3$ is larger than 1 because $3/3$ is equal to 1)

- Understanding that fractions "missing one piece" are ordered inversely to the size of the missing piece (for example, $2/3$ is smaller than $3/4$ because the $1/3$ missing is larger than the $1/4$ missing)

- Identifying equivalent fractions

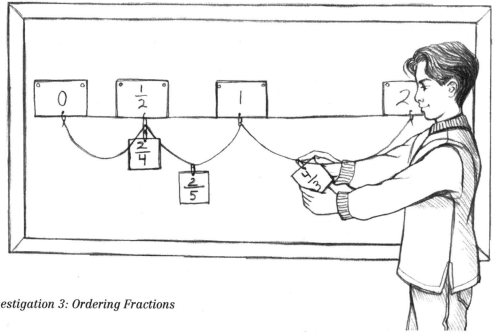

What to Plan Ahead of Time

Materials

- Oak tag for fraction cards—15 letter-size sheets per deck (use colored oak tag and a different color for each deck, if possible): 1 class deck and 1 deck per group of 4 students (Sessions 1–2)

- Oak tag for landmark cards—2 letter-size sheets per set: 2 class sets and 1 set per group of 4 students (Sessions 3, 4, 5)

- Tape (Sessions 4–5)

- Overhead projector, transparencies, and pens (Sessions 1, 2, and 3)

- Scissors: 1 per group of 4 students (Sessions 1–2)

- Glue sticks: 1 per group of 4 students (Sessions 1–2)

- 2 sturdy pieces of yarn or string (each about 15 feet) and 70 paper clips for 2 class number lines (Sessions 4–5)

Other Preparation

- Duplicate student sheets and teaching resources (located at the end of this unit) in the following quantities. If you have Student Activity Booklets, copy only the transparency marked with an asterisk.

For Sessions 1–2

Fractions for Fraction Cards (p. 79): 1 per group of 4 students

Blank Wholes for Fraction Cards (p. 80): 6 per group of 4 students.

How to Play Fraction Fish (p. 81): 1 per student

Fraction Cards for Playing Fraction Fish (p. 82): 1 per student

For Session 3

Student Sheet 14, Fractions in Containers (p. 77): 1 per student (homework)

Table for Grouping Fractions Between Landmarks* (p. 83): 1 overhead transparency

For Sessions 4–5

How to Play Capture Fractions (p. 84): 1 per student

Student Sheet 15, Comparing Fractions (p. 78): 1 per student

- Make fraction cards for 2/3 and 13/4. Cut out three blank wholes from the Teaching Resource, Blank Wholes for Fraction Cards (p. 80). Color 2/3 of one blank whole, paste it onto a 41/4" by 51/2" piece of oak tag, and label the card: 2/3. Then color one blank whole and 3/4 of another, paste both onto a piece of oak tag, and label the card with the number 13/4. (Sessions 1–2)

- Make sets of landmark cards by writing the numbers 0, 1/2, 1, and 2 on pieces of oak tag, one number per piece. (Sessions 3–5)

- Punch holes near the top and bottom center of each card in the class deck of fraction cards and in the bottom center of two sets of landmark cards. Put unbent paper clips through the top hole to clip the cards to the line. Equivalent fractions hang by paper clips from one another. (Sessions 4–5)

- Hang the strings for two separate fraction clotheslines. Attach landmark cards for 0, 1/2, 1, 2 to the strings according to their distance apart (for example, make 2 twice as far from 1 as 1 is from 1/2). (Sessions 4–5)

Making Fraction Cards

Materials

- Oak tag for fraction cards
- Fractions for Fraction Cards (1 per group of 4)
- Blank Wholes for Fraction Cards (6 per group of 4)
- Scissors (1 for every group)
- Glue sticks (1 for every group)
- How to Play Fraction Fish (1 per student)
- Fraction Cards for Playing Fraction Fish (1 per student)
- Overhead projector
- Blank transparencies (optional)

What Happens

Each group of four students makes a deck of 60 fraction cards on which they create visual representations of fractions, including fractions greater than 1. Collaboratively, they make a class deck that they will use to create two ordered fraction clotheslines. The class learns to play the game Fraction Fish to practice finding equivalent fractions. Their work focuses on:

- developing visual representations of fractions, including fractions greater than 1
- understanding the numerical representation of fractions greater than 1 (for example, $4/3$ is the same as $3/3 + 1/3$, which is the same as $11/3$)
- recognizing equivalence of fractions such as $1/2$ and $2/4$ both visually and numerically

 Ten-Minute Math: Guess My Number   Continue to do Guess My Number outside math class. This time pick a fraction or a group of fractions and give the students one or more clues. If students have completed their fraction cards, encourage them to use the cards to help them guess the number.

You might start by thinking about one-third and saying the following:

I am thinking of a fraction. It is smaller than one-half. Talk with your partner to decide what fraction it could be.

There are infinite possibilities such as $1/5$, $2/5$, and $8/17$. Students will most likely guess one of the fractions they have used: $1/3$, $1/4$, $1/6$, $1/8$, $1/12$. Write all their answers. Have students ask questions to narrow down the answer. As you give responses to their questions, ask them which fractions have become eliminated and cross those out.

Repeat this process with seven-eighths in mind.

I am thinking of a fraction. It is larger than one-half. It is smaller than one whole. What fraction could it be?

(Again there are infinite answers, such as $2/3$, $4/5$, and $51/100$. The most familiar is $3/4$.)

As students become more practiced, try varying the conditions of the fraction you are thinking of.

I am thinking of a fraction. It can be broken into fourths. It is between one whole and two wholes.

(The answer could be 1 1/4, 1 1/2, or 1 3/4)

For variations of Guess My Number, see p. 56.

Making Fraction Cards

Introducing Fraction Cards Divide students into groups of four. If you can't make groups of four evenly, make sure each group has at least three students in it. To each group, pass out one copy of Fractions for Fraction Cards and six copies of Blank Wholes for Fraction Cards.

For the next two days, each group is going to make a deck of fraction cards.

Show students how to make a fraction card, using as examples the ones for 2/3 and 1 3/4 that you prepared. Each group of students will make cards with both visual and numerical representations for all the numbers on the Fractions for Fraction Cards sheet. When students have finished, there will be five to eight full decks of fraction cards in the classroom, depending on the size of the class. While students have been making unusual pictures of fractions for the previous several sessions, it is important that on the fraction cards, they use simple rectangular representations so that it will be easy for them to order the representations. For example, fourths can be illustrated as shown below in the square at the far right or as four parallel stripes similar to the thirds:

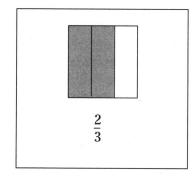
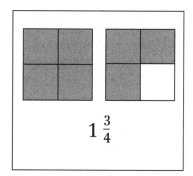

$$\frac{2}{3} \qquad\qquad 1\frac{3}{4}$$

Two Finished Fraction Cards

This may be the first time many students have worked with fractions greater than one whole. Before the class starts to work on the fraction cards, discuss the visual representation for fractions greater than 1.

How could you make a picture for the fraction 3/2?

Be sure students understand the idea of a number being made up of a whole and some fraction that is less than 1. Questions such as these can help:

Is 3/2 more or less than 1? How do you know?

If you split 3 things between 2 people, how much would each person get? What name might you give to that portion? What are some other ways to write 3/2 as a fraction? (If students don't come up with 1½ themselves, introduce this mixed number to represent 3/2.)

What are some other ways to write 1 as a fraction? (2/2, 3/3, 4/4, . . .)

Name another fraction greater than 1. How would we draw a picture for it?

Name and draw pictures for some fractions that are larger than 2.

Making Fraction Cards Groups work collaboratively to make their decks of fraction cards. As they do each card, they cross off that fraction on the Fractions for Fraction Cards sheet. Students check their partitioning and shading of the small squares with one another before gluing them to the cards. In cases where students in the group disagree about how a fraction can be illustrated, they should come to you as arbiter. It is important that their pictures are correct, since they will be using the cards to make judgments about equivalence and ordering of fractions.

Groups need to be able to recognize their decks of cards once they are made. If you have not provided different colors of oak tag for each group's deck, each group should mark all the backs of the cards in their deck with an identifying mark or colored scribble to differentiate them from those of the other decks in the class.

In addition to the decks the groups make, you will need a class deck for the next session. As groups finish their own decks, they can make cards for the class deck. You may wish to assign a column of fractions to each group. Choose a different identifying mark for the back of the class deck and remind students to mark cards in the class deck with it.

As you circulate among the groups making cards, watch for problems students might have using wholes. The introduction of fractions greater than 1 can confuse students, even if they were competent in their previous work with fractions less than 1. See the **Teacher Note**, Problems with Wholes (p. 44).

Recognizing Equivalent Fractions

While students may have noticed in the previous investigations that some fractions with different names have the same area (for example, 2/6 and 1/3), they have not worked in an organized way with equivalent fractions. The next activity gives them the opportunity to "see" the equivalence between such fractions by looking at their representations.

When all the decks are complete, have each group place their cards face up on their workspace so they can see as many as possible. Write 2/4 on the board or on an overhead transparency and invite a student to draw or describe an illustration for it. Challenge groups to find fractions with different names that have the same amount of area as 2/4. A student from a group that has found one comes to the board, writes the equivalent fraction, draws an illustration for it, and explains why it is the same as 2/4. Repeat this exercise for some of these fractions:

$$\frac{3}{3} \quad \frac{1}{3} \quad \frac{1}{4} \quad \frac{4}{6} \quad \frac{2}{12} \quad \frac{0}{3} \quad \frac{3}{2}$$

The point of this activity is to notice the equivalence of pictorial representations that cover the same amount of area, even though one representation is divided into twice or three times as many spaces as the other. Some students may also notice the numerical patterns that identify equivalent fractions (for example, $1/3 = 2/6$ because $1 \times 2 = 2$ and $3 \times 2 = 6$). This is, of course, a valid way to identify equivalent fractions. Be sure, however, that students can explain why. See the **Teacher Note**, Visualizing Equivalent Fractions (p. 45).

Playing Fraction Fish

This fractions activity was developed by a fourth-grade class during our field test. It gives students additional experience identifying equivalent fractions. The object of the game is to make matches of equivalent fraction cards and to obtain the most cards in their "captured fish" pile. For a complete set of instructions, refer to How to Play Fraction Fish (p. 81). Demonstrate the game by playing it with two or three other students using one deck of fraction cards. Be sure the rest of the class can see each match. Students play this game for any time remaining in Session 2 and for homework.

Sessions 1 and 2 Follow-Up

Playing Fraction Fish   Students take home How to Play Fraction Fish (p. 81) and Fraction Cards for Playing Fraction Fish (p. 82) in order to play Fraction Fish with someone at home. Remind students to keep the fractions cards from this game in a safe place at home; they will use the cards for homework in Sessions 4–5.

Homework

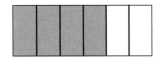
When students are trying to work with fractions both under and over 1 at the same time, they sometimes get confused about what to think of as the whole. In representing a number over 1, for example, they may try to represent the ratio within a single whole. For example, Lesley Ann drew $4/3$ like this:

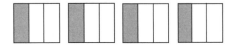

Lesley Ann's $4/3$

Lesley Ann: Well, I did $4/3$'s. And I had two pieces stuck together.

Here Lesley Ann was stumped by the need to have four pieces shaded when thirds only provide three in a single whole. Her solution was to combine two wholes to get enough thirds. Had she kept the two wholes separate, her solution would have been correct.

Some students make more wholes than necessary, rather than fewer. Joey represented $4/3$ like this:

Joey's $4/3$

Here, Joey may have been thinking about creating four squares, each showing $1/3$, for a total of four-thirds. Again, this solution is correct, but confusing. He did not realize he could combine three of the thirds into a whole.

Another example is Luisa's rendition of $1/5$.

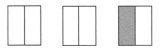

Luisa's $1/5$

It is not clear whether Luisa means to have one out of five sections colored (if you don't count the uncolored half of the third square), or if she means to represent the numerator by the one colored section and the denominator by the five uncolored sections. Neither of these represents one-fifth of one.

These problems do not usually emerge when students are working only with fractions under 1, but these kinds of responses may uncover students' lack of clarity about the role of wholes in representing fractions.

Visualizing Equivalent Fractions

It is often quite easy to turn one equivalent fraction into another, either by adding or removing a line. For example, you can show that 1/3 = 2/6 with the following pictures:

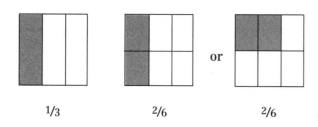

1/3   2/6   or   2/6

The first two fraction representations are the same, with the exception of the horizontal line, so it is easy to see that the same amount of area is colored in the two pictures. The only difference is the name we give to the fraction. If there are 3 pieces in the whole, 1 is colored. If there are 6 pieces, 2 are colored. One way to demonstrate this equivalence is by drawing the picture for one-third and drawing in the horizontal line that makes it two-sixths. Or you can draw the picture for two-sixths and erase the horizontal line, arriving at the representation for one-third. This simple demonstration is not as clear if two-sixths is drawn with two sections colored on the top row, as in the third picture shown, but students may explain that they could move the second square on the top to the bottom left corner so the picture would look like the picture of one-third. Similar demonstrations can be done with 1/2 and 2/4, 1/2 and 3/6 (there are two extra lines that make the difference between the two pictures 1/2 and 3/6), 2/3 and 4/6, and so on.

It is important that students can explain without the pictures in front of them why pairs of fractions are equivalent. For example, a student might point out that when the denominator is twice as big, the pieces are half the size, so you have to take twice as many; sixths are half as big as thirds, so you need two of them to equal one-third. When the denominator is three times as big (as in three-sixths compared to one-half), the pieces are only one third the size, so you must take three times as many pieces to have as much.

Ordering Fractions with Respect to Landmarks

Materials

- Student Sheet 14 (1 per student, homework)
- Transparency of Table for Grouping Fractions Between Landmarks
- Overhead projector
- Fraction cards (1 deck per group)
- Landmark cards (1 set per group)

What Happens

Groups of students sort their decks of fraction cards with respect to the landmarks 0, 1/2, 1, and 2. They discuss discrepancies among groups' sortings and decide as a class which sorting is correct. Their work focuses on:

- comparing fractions with the landmarks 0, 1/2, 1, and 2
- discriminating among fractions less than and greater than 1

Activity

Groups Order Fractions with Respect to Landmarks

When each group has finished making its deck of fraction cards and the class deck is also complete, pass out to each group one set of landmark cards with 0, 1/2, 1, and 2 (see instructions for making landmark cards on p. 39). Each group lays out its landmark cards in order on the floor or on several desks pushed together, leaving space between each pair for piles of other cards. Remind students about the concept of landmarks.

When else did you use landmarks this year? What numbers were those landmarks? (In the landmarks unit, 10, 25, 50, and 100 were among the landmark numbers.) **How are these numbers—0, 1/2, 1, and 2—similar to the other landmarks? How are they different?**

Groups of students place each card in their decks in piles *between* the landmarks or *on* or *underneath* the landmarks; there will be seven piles:

- equal to 0
- between 0 and 1/2
- equal to 1/2
- between 1/2 and 1
- equal to 1
- between 1 and 2
- equal to 2 or greater than 2

Placing their cards between landmarks requires students to compare many fractions with 1/2. Several kinds of mathematical reasoning come into play in these comparisons; the **Teacher Note**, Comparing Fractions to 1/2 (p. 48), has several examples of students' work.

Taking a Poll After each team has divided its cards into seven piles, the members compare their results by counting the number of cards in each pile. You can use a transparency of the Table for Grouping Fractions Between Landmarks (p. 83) to record fractions in their correct column as the class agrees on them.

Collect data one column at a time since students will be rearranging their piles as they discuss their decisions with others. For each column, ask each group how many cards are in its pile. If all the groups agree, write down the fractions in that column. When you come to a column where groups disagree on the number of cards, stop to work on that pile. A group that disagrees with the others reads the cards in the pile aloud, and the other groups look through their piles to see if they agree. As students agree on a fraction, list it in the column. When students discover a fraction that is in one group's pile but not in another's, the class decides through discussion which placement is correct. Write the fraction in the column agreed on. Groups then rearrange their piles according to the class decision. After a pile has been discussed, students check that your list is correct. Move on to the next column, discuss it, and continue through the rest of the piles.

TABLE FOR GROUPING FRACTIONS BETWEEN LANDMARKS

= 0	between 0 and $\frac{1}{2}$	= $\frac{1}{2}$	between $\frac{1}{2}$ and 1	= 1	between 1 and 2	= 2 or greater than 2

Session 3 Follow-Up

 **Homework**

Fractions in Containers Assign Student Sheet 14, Fractions in Containers, for homework. Students write each fraction in the container representing the category where it belongs. The sheet is designed with five fractions in each category, so students can tell on their own if they have a fraction out of place.

❖ **Tip for the Linguistically Diverse Classroom** Read aloud the words under each container, as well as the rest of the directions on this page. Make sure limited English proficient students understand that the meanings of the words under the containers are also illustrated by the picture above them. Encourge students to refer to each drawing at home if they cannot yet read the words.

Teacher Note ▷ *Comparing Fractions to ¹/₂*

Students often use numerical thinking when comparing fractions to ¹/₂ because multiplying and dividing by 2 is relatively simple for them. For example, a student might conclude that ⁴/₇ is greater than ¹/₂ because ⁴/₇ × 2 is equal to ⁸/₇, which is bigger than 1. Another student compared ⁴/₇ and ¹/₂ this way: "One-half would be 3¹/₂ sevenths and 4 sevenths is bigger than 3¹/₂ sevenths." The same argument works for ²/₅ and ¹/₂: Two-fifths is smaller than ¹/₂ because ¹/₂ would be 2¹/₂ fifths.

The same kind of reasoning works for other numbers, primarily those with 1 as the numerator. A student argued that ¹/₄ was less than ²/₆ because one-quarter of 6 is 1¹/₂, so 1¹/₂ sixths is equal to 1 fourth and that is less than 2 sixths.

In the next session, students will compare pairs of fractions that lie between landmarks. Students are likely to use ¹/₂ as a landmark to compare two other fractions. Here is one student's justification for ⁵/₁₂ being larger than ¹/₃: "One-third means you need ¹/₂ of ¹/₃ to make it a half. But you'll need ¹/₁₂ to make ⁵/₁₂ a half. And ¹/₁₂ is smaller than ¹/₂ of ¹/₃, so ⁵/₁₂ is closer to ¹/₂. So ⁵/₁₂ is bigger."

Making a Fraction Number Line

What Happens

Working in small groups, students put together two fraction number lines, each of which contains half of the fraction cards in the class deck, by hanging the cards in order from a long clothesline. In parallel, students play Capture Fractions (a game in which the larger fraction wins each round) with the decks of fraction cards they have made. Their work focuses on:

- comparing the relative sizes of common fractions, including:

    unit fractions, such as 1/3 and 1/4

    fractions with the same denominator

    fractions with the same numerator

- comparing any fraction with 1/2 and with 1

- comparing fractions that are missing one piece of a whole, such as 3/4 and 5/6

Materials

- Yarn or string (2 sturdy pieces about 15 feet long)
- 70 paper clips
- Fraction cards (1 deck per group)
- Landmark cards (2 sets)
- Tape
- How to Play Capture Fractions
- Student Sheet 15 (1 per student for assessment)

Activity

Students use their fraction cards to play Capture Fractions, a game modeled on the card game War, in which the larger fraction wins each round. The game can be played by any number of students, but gets complicated when more than three play because it requires comparing four or more fractions. Distribute to each student How to Play Capture Fractions, which gives instructions for playing the game.

Demonstrate a game between yourself and a student or with two students in front of the class. Decide as a class who wins each round, and play a few rounds until the sequence becomes clear. Then the entire class divides into pairs (with one possible set of three if you have an odd number of students) and each pair plays with 30 cards (half of their group's deck). Students may switch partners after a few rounds.

Students may want to play Capture Fractions other times during the day. If only a few students are playing, pairs may play with full decks of 60 cards.

Playing Capture Fractions

Making a Fraction Number Line

Prior to this activity, hang the strings for two number lines and attach to them the landmark cards. Students will make each fraction number line using half of the cards in the class deck. Making a single number line with 60 cards is conceptually and logistically difficult; splitting the deck in two makes the task more accessible for fourth graders.

Invite two groups of students to work on the number lines. The rest of the class can continue to play Capture Fractions. The first two groups can hang all the cards equal to the landmark numbers. If a fraction to be added is the same as a fraction that is already on the clothesline, it should be hung below the equivalent fraction by inserting the paper clip in the bottom hole of the card already on the line. For example, 2/4 should be hung from the landmark 1/2; and when a student wants to place 3/6, he or she should hang 3/6 through the hole at the bottom of 2/4. The other cards can be kept in envelopes or held together with a rubber band. The next group can pick a task such as finding all the fractions between 0 and 1/2 or choosing any five to seven cards to add to the number line in the correct places.

You may want to invite your less-secure students to work early in the construction of the number line, since it becomes more difficult to place cards as more fractions are put on the line. See the **Teacher Note**, Strategies for Comparing Fractions (p. 52). Students placing the first cards between landmarks should try to put them in approximately the right place—closer to one end or the other. As more cards are added, cards can be moved to reflect more accurately the distances between fractions, since the paper clips slide on the string.

Assessment

Comparing Fractions

Student Sheet 15, Comparing Fractions, provides an assessment based on the ideas explored during Investigation 3. The following problems are included. Hand out the sheet for students to work on by themselves.

1. Circle the larger fraction in each pair. Write = if you think they are the same size. Next to each pair, show or write about how you decided.

   a. $\frac{3}{8}$ $\frac{1}{2}$

   b. $\frac{2}{3}$ $\frac{5}{6}$

   c. $\frac{3}{4}$ $\frac{4}{3}$

2. Put these fractions in order from smallest to largest. Use the clothesline below to order them.

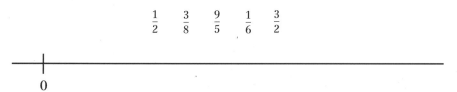

$$\frac{1}{2} \quad \frac{3}{8} \quad \frac{9}{5} \quad \frac{1}{6} \quad \frac{3}{2}$$

0

As students are working on problem 1 of this assessment, remind them to write explanations for which is the larger fraction in each of the pairs. Ask individuals having difficulty doing this how they compared the fractions. After they tell you, suggest they write down their ideas so you will understand when you read them later. For samples and explanations of students' responses to the problems above, see the **Teacher Note**, Assessment: Comparing Fractions (p. 53).

Activity

Choosing Student Work to Save

As the unit ends, you may want to use one of the following options for creating a record of students' work on this unit:

■ Students look back through their folders or notebooks and write about what they learned in this unit, what they remember most, what was hard or easy for them. You might have students do this work during their writing time.

■ Students select one or two pieces of their work as their best work. You also choose one or two pieces of their work to be saved in a portfolio for the year. You might include students' written solutions to the assessment, Proving Thirds and Sixths (Investigation 2, Session 3), and any other assessment tasks from this unit. Students can create a separate page with brief comments describing each piece of work.

■ You may want to send a selection of work home for parents to see. Students write cover letters, describing their work in this unit. This work should be returned if you are keeping a year-long portfolio of mathematics work for each student.

Sessions 4 and 5 Follow-Up

Playing Capture Fractions   For homework, students use the fraction cards they saved from the Session 1–2 homework in playing Capture Fractions with someone at home. Students will also need a copy of How to Play Capture Fractions.

 **Homework**

If your students are having trouble with some fraction comparisons, you might want to use a set of examples that would lead them to some of the following strategies, expressed below in students' words.

■ Comparing whether the denominator is the same

Example: 3/4 and 2/4

"That's easy. All the pieces are the same size. So if you have 3, of course it's more than 2."

■ Comparing whether the numerator is the same

Example: 9/12 and 9/4

"Nine-twelfths is less than nine-fourths because 4 pieces is less than 12, so the fourths are lots bigger than the twelfths."

"There are 2 wholes in nine-fourths, with some still left over, and nine-twelfths isn't even 1."

■ Noticing equivalent fractions by manipulating pictures

Example: Joey has 4/10, in the following configuration:

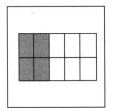

"I have four-tenths, so this would be two-fifths because if the line in the middle wasn't here, it would be the same picture as two-fifths."

■ Comparing how far fractions are from a landmark, combined with some of the strategies above

Example: 9/12 and 6/9

"They can't be the same because if you split a square into twelfths you have to have very small pieces. But with ninths, the pieces will still be small, but they'll be bigger. If you have 3 left over of ninths they'll be bigger than 3 left over on nine-twelfths. So nine-twelfths is bigger than six-ninths because it's closer to 1."

■ Finding a third fraction that is equal to one fraction and less than the other fraction

Example: 5/12 and 1/3

"Five-twelfths is bigger. This whole is 4 pieces and 4 pieces and 4 pieces. So four-twelfths is equal to one-third. But then five-twelfths still has a part left, so it's bigger than one-third."

Assessment: Comparing Fractions

As you observe students working on the problems on Student Sheet 15 and look over their solutions, you may get a sense of the ways each student approaches fractions and what strengths and weaknesses each may have. Use the following questions to guide your observations:

- Do students use pictorial strategies, numerical strategies, or a mixture?
- Can they use fraction landmarks, such as $1/2$ and 1, to compare fractions?
- Do they know how to differentiate among fractions that are "missing one piece"?
- Can they recognize fractions greater than 1?

1a. The first problem on Student Sheet 15 lets you see how students think about comparing $1/2$ with other fractions. Reasoning in terms of pictures often focuses on the missing $1/8$ that makes $3/8$ to be less than $1/2$.

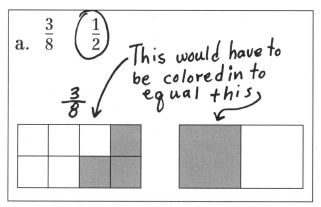

Numerical reasoning on this problem comes from knowing that 4 is $1/2$ of 8:

a. $\frac{3}{8}$ $\boxed{\frac{1}{2}}$

Three is less than half of 8.

Some students both draw pictures and write numerical representations of the quantities in their pictures.

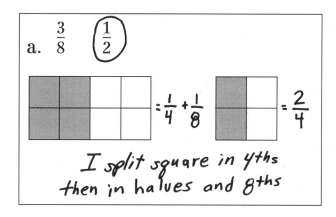

Look out for correct answers based on limited understanding, as in thinking any fractions can be compared by looking only at their denominators, so that, for example, a fraction with a denominator of 2 is always larger than a fraction with a denominator of 8. Students tend to learn the "backwards rule" (the smaller the denominator, the larger the fraction) when they are working only with fractions that have a numerator of 1 and then generalize the rule to other fractions.

a. $\frac{3}{8}$ $\boxed{\frac{1}{2}}$

2 is smaller than 8 so in fractions it's bigger.

Continued on next page

1b. The second problem focuses on students' concepts about fractions that are "missing one piece" in comparison with 1. A useful strategy students adopt is to focus on the size of the missing piece, either numerically:

b. $\frac{2}{3}$ $\boxed{\frac{5}{6}}$

6th's are smaller than 3th's

$\frac{5}{6}$ is bigger because it has less space not colored in.

or pictorially:

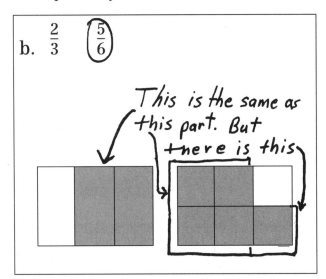

b. $\frac{2}{3}$ $\boxed{\frac{5}{6}}$

This is the same as this part. But there is this

This requires several steps of thinking and inverse reasoning. Some students may still have the misconception that all fractions that have one piece "not colored" are the same. This student, for example, has not yet understood that the size of the missing piece is crucial to the comparison.

"I would say equal. One space is not colored. Like two-thirds, three-fourths, five-sixths, seven-eighths."

1c. The third problem focuses on students' conceptions of fractions over 1. Many students will answer this by pointing out that 4/3 is more than a whole, while 3/4 is less. Some students may give the right answer but the wrong reason:

"Four-thirds is bigger because this has 4 colored, and the other has 3 colored."

2. Looking at the way students put numbers on the clothesline allows you to see whether or not they use landmarks to order fractions. This student adds the landmarks 1/2, 1, and 2 to the fraction clothesline before placing the other fractions on it.

2. Put these fractions in order from smallest to largest. Use the clothesline below to order them:

$$\frac{1}{2} \qquad \frac{3}{8} \qquad \frac{9}{5} \qquad \frac{1}{6} \qquad \frac{3}{2}$$

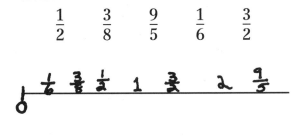

It seems that he then related each fraction to one of the landmarks: one-sixth is a little larger than 0, three-eighths is a little smaller than one-half, three halves is a little larger than one.

You can also see from this problem whether students can order fractions above 1. Many students order the fractions below 1 successfully but have trouble with 9/5 and 3/2. Notice if students have placed these two fractions at the end of the ordering. This may mean that they know that both 9/5 and 3/2 are greater than 1 but do not know how to compare them. Notice that this student put 9/5 to the right of 2 instead of 1, and he did not try to place 3/2 exactly. He recognized which fractions are larger than 1, but he did not work out what mixed numbers they equal.

Guess My Number

Basic Activity

You choose a number for students to guess. Then, start by giving a series of clues about the characteristics of the number. For example: It is less than 50. It is a multiple of 7. One of its digits is 2 more than the other digit.

Students work in pairs to try to identify the number. Record students' suggested solutions on the board and invite them to challenge any solutions they don't agree with. If more than one solution fits the clues, encourage students to ask more questions to narrow the field. They might ask, for example: Is the number less than 40? Is the number a multiple of 5?

Guess My Number involves students in logical reasoning as they apply the clues to choose numbers that fit and eliminate those that don't. Students also investigate aspects of number theory as they learn to recognize and describe the characteristics of numbers and relationships among numbers. Students' work focuses on:

- systematically eliminating possibilities
- using evidence
- formulating questions to logically eliminate possible solutions
- recognizing relationships among numbers, such as identifying multiples or factors of each other
- learning to use mathematical terms that describe numbers

Materials

- 100 chart (or 300 chart, when a larger range of numbers is being considered) (optional)
- Scraps of paper or numeral cards for showing solutions (optional)
- Calculators (for variation)

Procedure

Step 1. Choose a number. You may want to write it down so that you don't forget what you picked!

Step 2. Give students clues. Sometimes, you might choose clues so that only one solution is possible. Other times, you might choose clues so that several solutions are possible. Use clues that describe number characteristics and relationships, such as factors, multiples, the number of digits, and odd and even.

Step 3. Students work in pairs to find numbers that fit the clues. A 100 chart (or 300 chart for larger numbers) and scraps of paper or numeral cards are useful for recording numbers they think might fit. Give students just one or two minutes to find numbers they think might work.

Step 4. Record all suggested solutions. To get responses from every student, you may want to ask students to record their solutions on scraps of paper and hold them up on a given signal. Some teachers provide numeral cards that students can hold up to show their solution (for example, they might hold up a 2 and a 1 together to show 21). List on the board all solutions that students propose. Students look over all the proposed solutions and challenge any they think don't fit all the clues. They should give the reasons for their challenges.

Step 5. Invite students to ask further questions. If more than one solution fits all the clues, let students ask yes-or-no questions to try to eliminate some of the possibilities, until only one solution remains. You can erase numbers as students' questions eliminate them (be sure to ask students to tell you which numbers you should erase). Encourage students to ask questions that might eliminate more than one of the proposed solutions.

Continued on next page

Guess My Number Variations

New Number Characteristics During the year, vary this game to include mathematical terms that describe numbers or relationships among numbers that have come up in mathematics class. For example, include factors, multiples, doubling (tripling, halving), square numbers, prime numbers, odd and even numbers, less than and more than concepts, as well as the number of digits in a number.

Large Numbers Begin with numbers under 100, but gradually expand the range of numbers that you include in your clues to larger numbers with which your students have been working. For example:

- It is a multiple of 50.
- It has 3 digits.
- Two of its digits are the same.
- It is not a multiple of 100.

Guess My Fraction Pick a fraction. Tell students whether it is smaller than one-half, between one-half and one, between one and two, or bound by any other familiar numbers. You might use clues like these:

- It is a multiple of one-fourth (for example, one-half, three-fourths, one whole, one and one-fourth).
- The numerator is 2 (for example, two-thirds, two-fifths).
- You can make it with pattern blocks (for example, two-thirds, five-sixths).

Don't Share Solutions Until the End As students become more practiced in formulating questions to eliminate possible solutions, you may want to skip step 4. That is, student pairs find all solutions they think are possible, but these are not shared and posted. Rather, in a whole-class discussion, students ask yes-or-no questions, but privately eliminate numbers on

their own list of solutions. When students have no more questions, they volunteer their solutions and explain why they think their answer is correct.

Calculator Guess My Number Present clues that provide opportunities for computation using a calculator. For example:

- It is larger than 35×20.
- It is smaller than $1800 \div 20$.
- It is smaller than $1800 \div 2$.
- One of its factors is 25.
- None of its digits is 7.

Related Homework Options

Guess My Number Homework Prepare a sheet with one or two Guess My Number problems for students to work on at home. As part of their work, students should write whether they think only one number fits the clues or whether several numbers fit. If only one solution exists, how do they know it is the only number that fits the clues? If more than one solution is possible, do they think they have them all? How do they know?

Students' Secret Numbers Each student chooses a number and develops clues to present to the rest of the class. You'll probably want to have students submit their numbers and clues to you for review in advance. If the clues are too broad (for example, 50 solutions are possible) or don't work, ask the students to revise their clues. Once you approve the clues, students are in charge of presenting them, running the discussion, and answering all questions about their number during a Ten-Minute Math session.

The following activities will help ensure that this unit is comprehensible to students who are acquiring English as a second language. The suggested approach is based on *The Natural Approach: Language Acquisition in the Classroom* by Stephen D. Krashen and Tracy D. Terrell (Alemany Press, 1983). The intent is for second-language learners to acquire new vocabulary in an active, meaningful context.

Note that *acquiring* a word is different from *learning* a word. Depending on their level of proficiency, students may be able to comprehend a word upon hearing it during an investigation, without being able to say it. Other students may be able to use the word orally, but not read or write it. The goal is to help students naturally acquire targeted vocabulary at their present level of proficiency.

We suggest using these activities just before the related investigations. The activities can also be led by English-proficient students.

Investigations 1-3

cake, flag, quilt, colored

1. Make a quick outline of a cake, a flag, and a quilt on the chalkboard. Point to and identify each drawing as you pantomime a related action (for example: take a taste of the cake, salute the flag, cover yourself with the quilt).

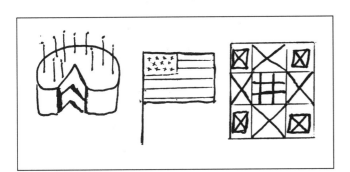

2. Point to the unshaded area of each drawing as you explain that the cake, the flag, and the quilt are not colored. Use a piece of chalk to fill in half of the area of each drawing. Tell students that half of the cake, the flag, and the quilt are now colored.

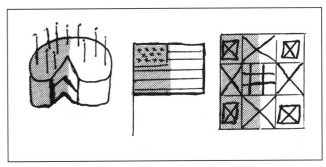

3. Ask student volunteers to color in the remaining part of each drawing on the chalkboard. When they are finished, point to the filled-in areas as you explain that each drawing has been completely colored.

4. Challenge students' comprehension of these vocabulary words by creating action commands, such as:

   Draw a cake, but do not color it.

   Draw a flag and color half of it.

   Draw a quilt and color just two of its squares.

Blackline Masters

Dear Family,

In math, our class is starting a new unit called *Different Shapes, Equal Pieces*. This unit helps students learn about fractions by thinking about different parts of squares, rectangles, and other shapes. By looking at areas, children can figure out which fractions are the same or which of two fractions is larger. Being able to "see" fractions this way helps in combining them, in finding the difference between one and another, and in figuring out what combinations of fractions would cover a whole shape. An important thing students will learn is this: If you're looking at a certain area, like the top of a cake, you can make it into fourths (or other fractions) in many different ways. The important thing is that each fourth has to cover the same amount of space. They don't have to be the same shape, but they each have to cover exactly one-fourth of the space. While this may seem obvious, in many textbooks students see shapes already divided into fractions and never have a chance to divide up areas on their own. In this unit, students get plenty of opportunity to make their own fractions.

Both in class and at home, students will work on problems like this: Divide a square into halves in several different ways. Make sure that in some of your ways, the two halves are not the same shape. These are the kinds of halves that students often come up with. Notice that the third square is divided into halves that are the same size but different shapes.

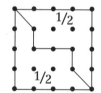 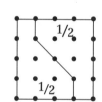 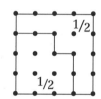

You can help your child by encouraging him or her to come up with more unusual divisions and to convince you that the squares are really divided in half (or into quarters, eighths, etc.). Children have interesting strategies for "proving" that the areas are the same. Watch for situations at home where similar thinking is relevant—for example, how can we split the driveway in equal amounts for shoveling snow; what are some different ways we can put cheese on half of the pizza?

In the second half of the unit, students will create a number clothesline to work on putting fractions in order. Their growing ability to form mental pictures of fractions will help them think about comparing fractions like 2/3 and 3/4. Talk with your child about these kinds of comparisons as they come up in your conversations together.

Sincerely,

Crazy Cakes for Two

Divide each of the "strange cakes" below into two equal halves.
The two halves do not need to have the same shape.

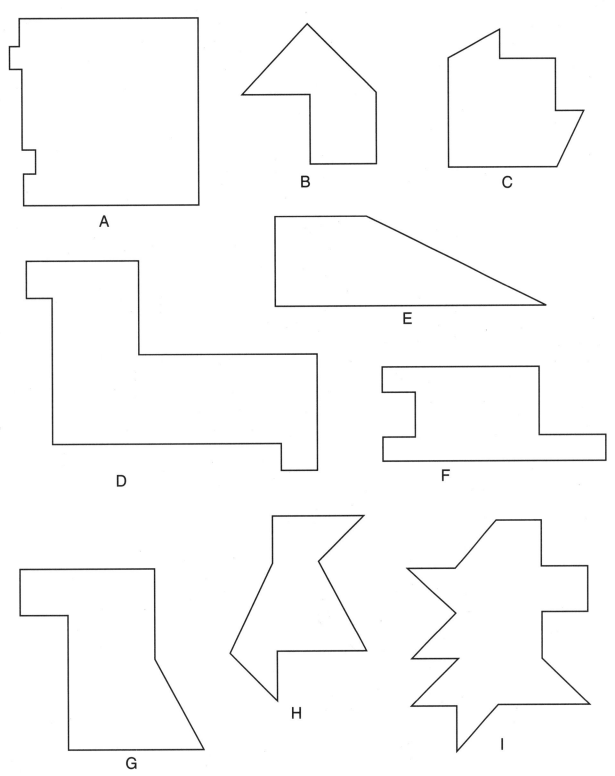

A

B

C

D

E

F

G

H

I

Dot-Paper Squares

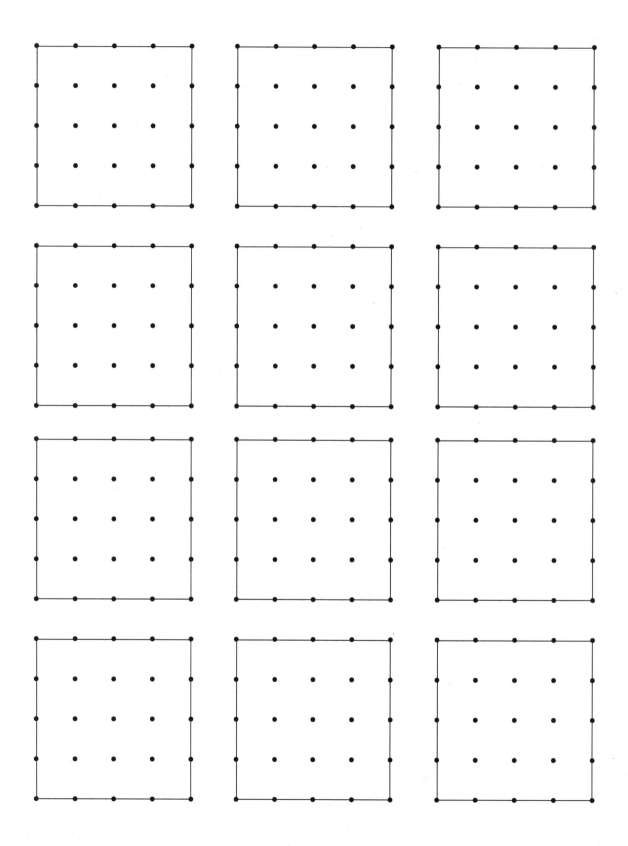

Proving Fractional Parts

1. Prove that this square is divided into halves.

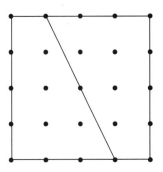

2. Prove that this square is divided into fourths.

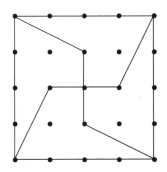

3. Prove that these two shapes have equal area.

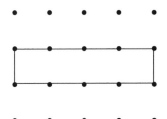 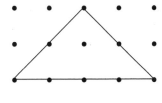

Squares for a Quilt of Fourths

Divide each small square into fourths in a different way.
Use your favorite fourths, or make up new ways of
dividing into fourths. Color each square's fourths right
after you divide it into four parts. Use the same four
colors.

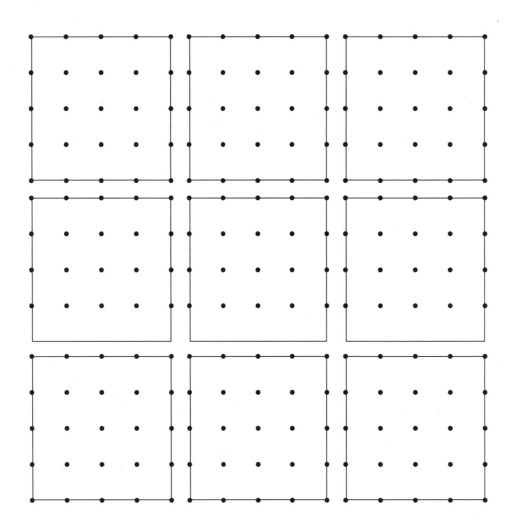

A Favorite Fourth

Draw one of your favorite or most interesting fourths.

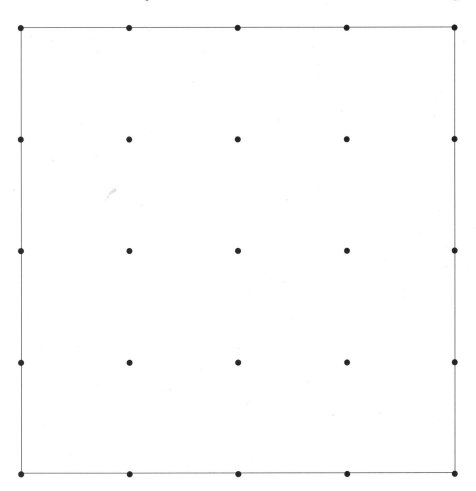

Use diagrams and/or words to prove that this square
is divided into fourths. Explain how you know that
each piece is one-fourth.

Large Dot Square for Combining Fractions

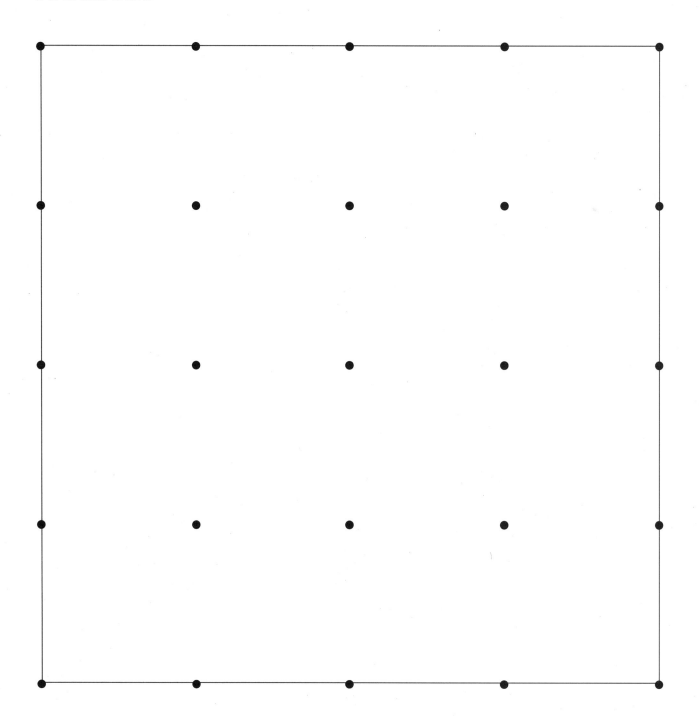

A Dot-Paper Square and Rectangle

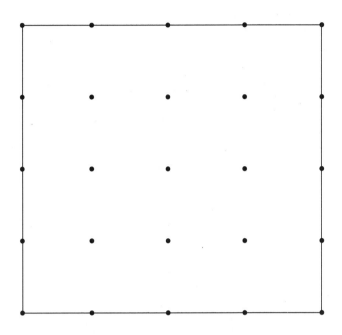

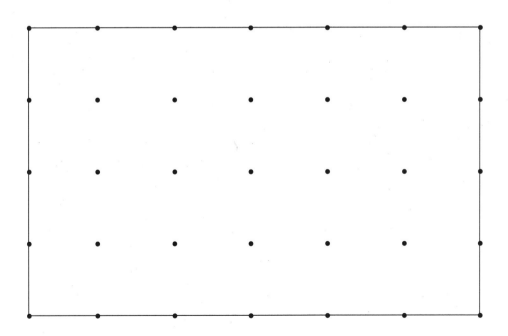

Dot-Paper Rectangles

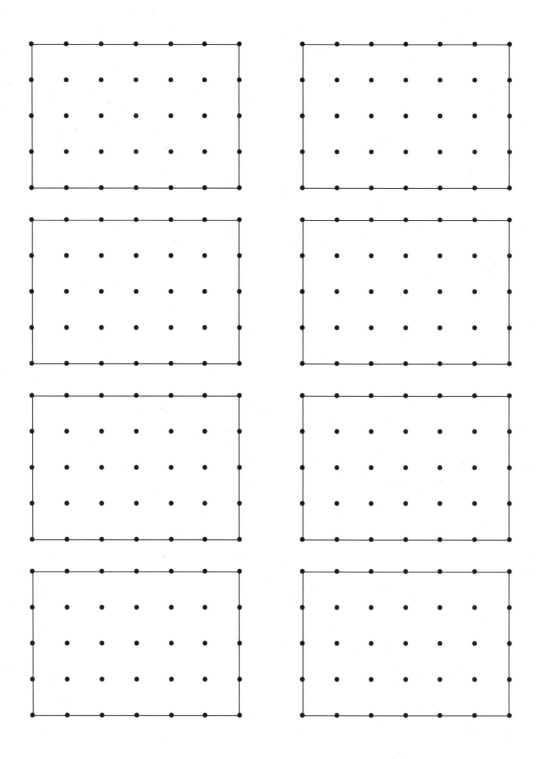

Thirds and Sixths

Divide this rectangle into thirds (3 equal parts).

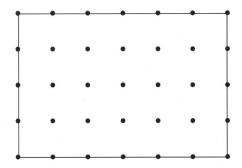

Explain how you know the rectangle is divided into thirds.

_____

Divide this rectangle into sixths (6 equal parts).

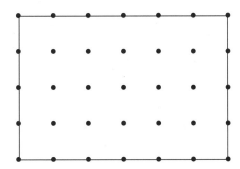

Explain how you know the rectangle is divided into sixths.

Proving Thirds and Sixths

1. Is this rectangle divided into thirds? Explain your answer.

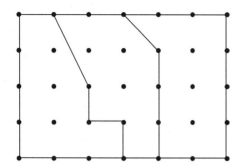

2. **a.** Is this rectangle divided into sixths? Explain your answer.

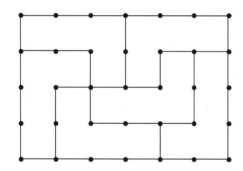

   b. Color one-third of the rectangle in 2a.
   Explain how you know it is one-third.

3. Some students say $\frac{1}{6}$ is larger than $\frac{1}{4}$
   because 6 is larger than 4.
   What do you think? Explain.

Large Dot Rectangle for Combining Fractions

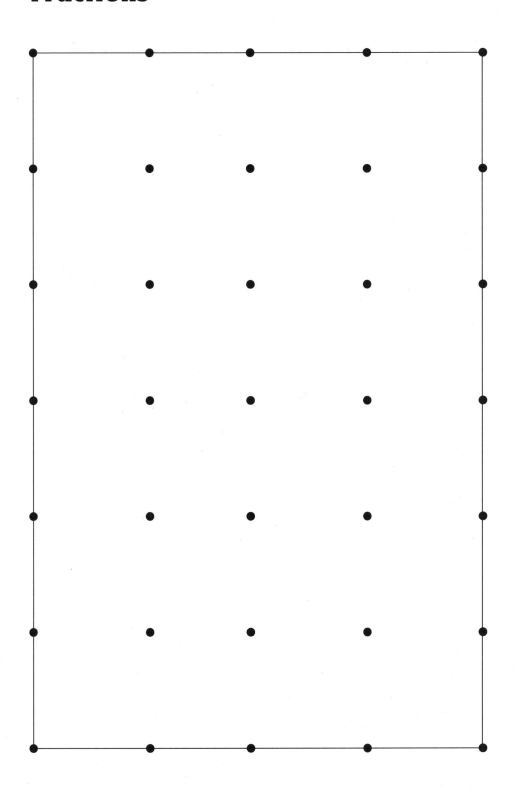

Blank Square (page 1 of 2)

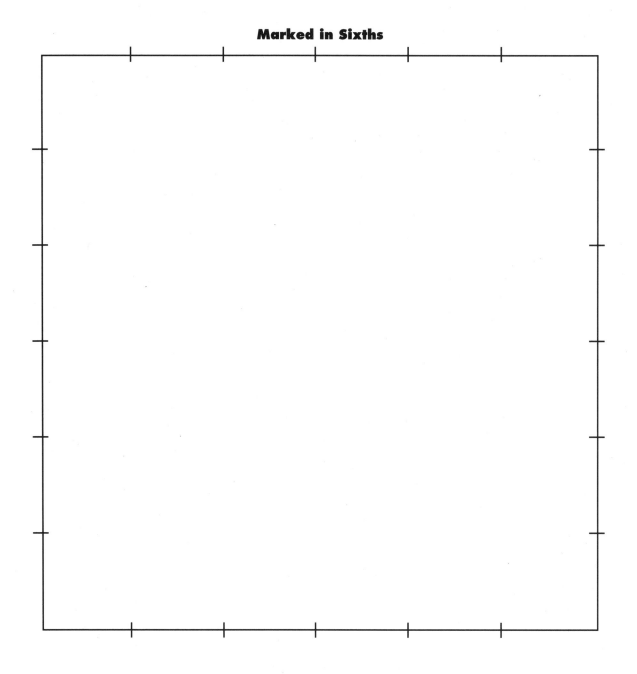

Marked in Sixths

Blank Square (page 2 of 2)

Marked in Eighths

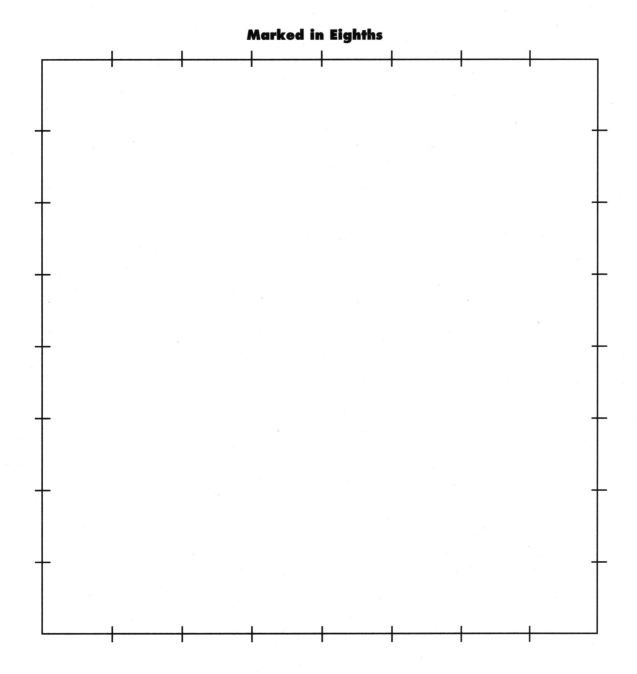

Agree or Disagree?

1. A fourth grader said that $\frac{3}{4}$ and $\frac{5}{6}$ are the same size
   because they both have one piece missing.
   Do you agree? Explain. Use pictures to make
   your argument clearer.

2. About how big is $\frac{4}{5}$ of this rectangle?
   Show your answer by shading in the rectangle.

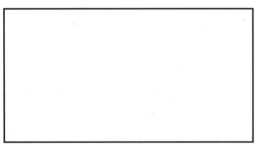

   What other fractions are near $\frac{4}{5}$ in size?

3. Which is larger, $\frac{2}{3}$ or $\frac{3}{2}$?
   Use words and pictures to explain your answer.

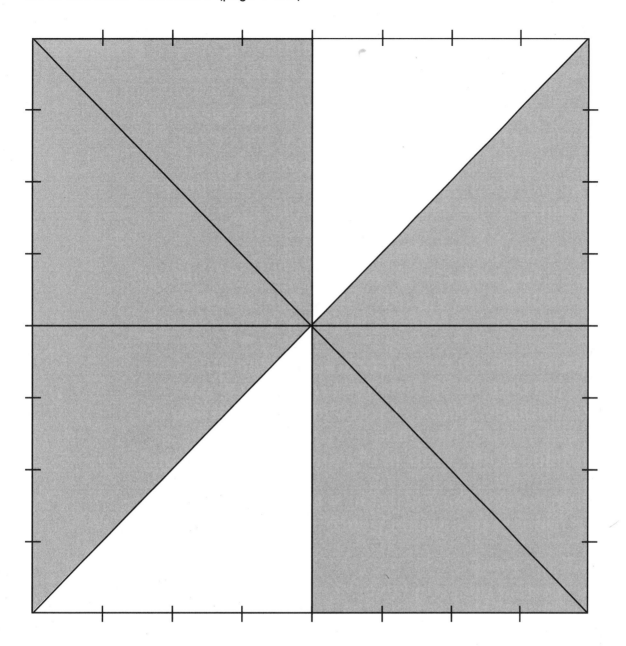

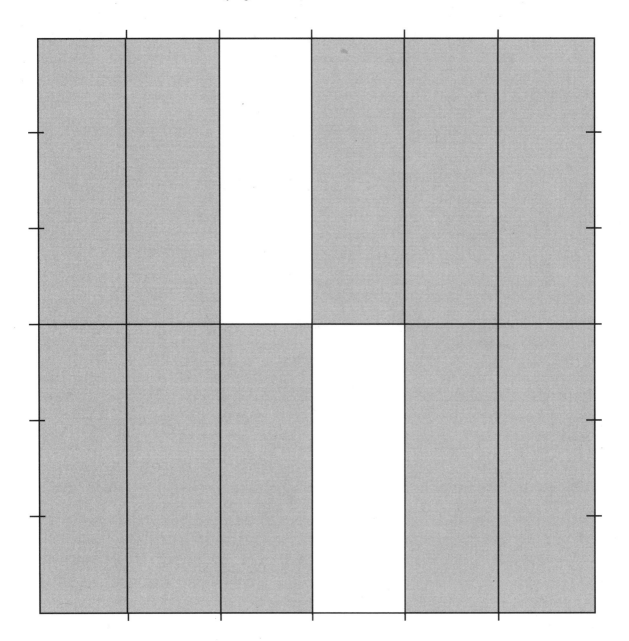

Fractions in Containers

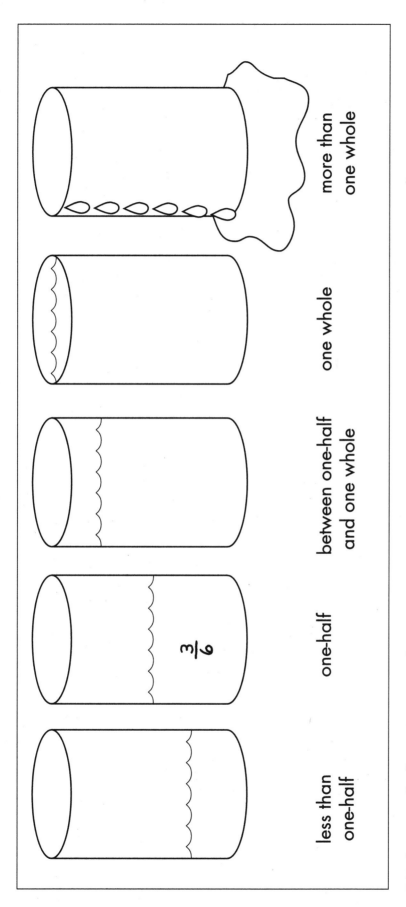

less than one-half

one-half

$\frac{3}{6}$

between one-half and one whole

one whole

more than one whole

Write each fraction in the container in which it belongs.

Cross out each fraction as you use it. ($\frac{3}{6}$ has been done for you.)

There are five fractions for each container.

$\cancel{\frac{3}{6}} \quad \frac{5}{5} \quad \frac{1}{4} \quad \frac{1}{5} \quad \frac{2}{3} \quad \frac{3}{5} \quad \frac{2}{2} \quad \frac{3}{2} \quad \frac{5}{7} \quad \frac{6}{3} \quad \frac{2}{5} \quad \frac{3}{4} \quad \frac{10}{20} \quad \frac{3}{10} \quad \frac{10}{5} \quad \frac{2}{6} \quad \frac{3}{2} \quad \frac{9}{10} \quad \frac{6}{5} \quad \frac{10}{10} \quad \frac{4}{8} \quad \frac{4}{5} \quad \frac{8}{8} \quad \frac{6}{12}$

Investigation 3 • Session 3
Different Shapes, Equal Pieces

Comparing Fractions

1. Circle the larger fraction in each pair.
   Write = if you think they are the same size.
   Next to each pair, show or write about how you decided.

   a. $\frac{3}{8}$ $\frac{1}{2}$

   b. $\frac{2}{3}$ $\frac{5}{6}$

   c. $\frac{3}{4}$ $\frac{4}{3}$

2. Put these fractions in order from smallest to largest.
   Use the clothesline below to order them.

   $\frac{1}{2}$ $\frac{3}{8}$ $\frac{9}{5}$ $\frac{1}{6}$ $\frac{3}{2}$

   0

$\frac{8}{4}$	$\frac{4}{2}$	$\frac{12}{12}$	$\frac{5}{3}$	$\frac{6}{3}$	$\frac{5}{8}$
$\frac{9}{4}$	$\frac{9}{6}$	$2\frac{1}{2}$	$\frac{10}{8}$	$1\frac{1}{3}$	$1\frac{3}{4}$
$1\frac{1}{2}$	$\frac{8}{3}$	$\frac{5}{2}$	$\frac{0}{2}$	$1\frac{2}{3}$	$\frac{2}{5}$
$\frac{3}{8}$	$\frac{0}{4}$	$\frac{7}{4}$	$\frac{4}{10}$	$\frac{8}{8}$	$\frac{0}{3}$
$\frac{4}{5}$	$\frac{4}{8}$	$\frac{4}{12}$	$\frac{5}{4}$	$\frac{6}{12}$	$\frac{1}{8}$
$\frac{0}{12}$	$\frac{6}{8}$	$\frac{6}{9}$	$\frac{2}{12}$	$\frac{8}{12}$	$\frac{2}{8}$
$\frac{7}{8}$	$1\frac{1}{4}$	$\frac{3}{12}$	$\frac{9}{12}$	$\frac{1}{2}$	$\frac{2}{3}$
$\frac{2}{4}$	$\frac{1}{6}$	$\frac{5}{6}$	$\frac{2}{2}$	$\frac{3}{3}$	$\frac{3}{4}$
$\frac{2}{6}$	$\frac{6}{6}$	$\frac{3}{2}$	$\frac{4}{3}$	$\frac{4}{4}$	$\frac{3}{6}$
$\frac{8}{6}$	$\frac{1}{3}$	$\frac{1}{4}$	$\frac{6}{4}$	$\frac{4}{6}$	$\frac{1}{5}$

Materials

Deck of Fraction Cards

Players: 2 or more

How to Play

1. Deal out 7 fraction cards to each player. The remaining fraction cards are placed in a deck in the center of the table.

2. Play proceeds around the circle. The object is to get cards from other players by matching a fraction card in their hands with one in your hand. Cards match if they are equivalent fractions (stand for the same amount). So, $\frac{2}{4}$ matches $\frac{1}{2}$, and $\frac{2}{3}$ matches $\frac{4}{6}$.

3. Each player in turn asks another player if he or she has an equivalent for a fraction, for example, $\frac{2}{4}$. If the second player has any fraction card worth the same amount, the first player gets that card and puts both cards in a "captured fish" pile. If the second player has more than one matching card, the first player gets all of them. If the second player has no matching cards, the first player has to "Fish!"—pick the top card in the face-down pile and add it to his or her hand. If this card results in a match, the player can, on the next turn, put the matching cards in the "captured fish" pile. In addition, the player may ask another player for a different match.

4. The game ends when a player has no more cards or when there are no more matches. In either case, the winner is the person with the most cards in his or her "captured fish" pile.

Use the fractions below to play Fraction Fish with someone at home. Cut the squares out and use them as cards.

$\dfrac{2}{3}$	$\dfrac{1}{6}$	$\dfrac{4}{2}$	$\dfrac{6}{6}$	$\dfrac{0}{2}$
$\dfrac{1}{4}$	$\dfrac{3}{6}$	$\dfrac{9}{6}$	$\dfrac{1}{8}$	$\dfrac{2}{4}$
1	$1\dfrac{1}{2}$	$\dfrac{4}{6}$	$\dfrac{6}{8}$	$\dfrac{0}{4}$
$\dfrac{4}{8}$	$\dfrac{8}{8}$	$\dfrac{8}{4}$	$\dfrac{6}{4}$	$\dfrac{4}{4}$
$\dfrac{6}{12}$	$\dfrac{0}{6}$	$\dfrac{1}{2}$	2	$\dfrac{3}{4}$

Investigation 3 • Resource
Different Shapes, Equal Pieces

TABLE FOR GROUPING FRACTIONS BETWEEN LANDMARKS

= 0	between 0 and $\frac{1}{2}$	= $\frac{1}{2}$	between $\frac{1}{2}$ and 1	= 1	between 1 and 2	= 2 or greater than 2

Materials

Deck of Fractions Cards

Players: 2 or more

How to Play

1. Divide the deck into equal-sized piles, one for each player. Players hold their piles upside down.

2. In each round, each player turns over the top card in his or her pile. The person with the largest fraction wins, takes the other players' cards, and puts them on the bottom of his or her own pile.

3. If two of the cards show equivalent fractions, those two players turn over another card. Whoever has the larger fraction wins all the other players' cards.

4. The person with the most cards wins. The game can be stopped at any time.

Practice Pages

This optional section provides homework ideas for teachers who want or need to give more homework than is assigned to accompany the activities in this unit. The problems included here provide additional practice in learning about number relationships and in solving computation and number problems. For number units, you may want to use some of these if your students need more work in these areas or if you want to assign daily homework. For other units, you can use these problems so that students can continue to work on developing number and computation sense while they are focusing on other mathematical content in class. We recommend that you introduce activities in class before assigning related problems for homework.

101 to 200 Bingo This game is introduced in the unit *Mathematical Thinking at Grade 4*. If your students are familiar with the game, you can simply send home the directions, game board, Tens Cards, and Numeral Cards so that students can play at home. If your students have not played the game before, introduce it in class and have students play once or twice before sending it home. You might have students do this activity two times for homework in this unit.

Ways to Count Money This type of problem is introduced in the unit *Mathematical Thinking at Grade 4*. Here, three problem sheets are provided. You can also make up other problems in this format, using numbers that are appropriate for your students. Students find two ways to solve each problem. They record their solution strategies.

Story Problems Story problems at various levels of difficulty are used throughout the *Investigations* curriculum. The three story problem sheets provided here help students review and maintain skills that have already been taught. You can also make up other problems in this format, using numbers and contexts that are appropriate for your students. Students solve the problems and then record their strategies.

How to Play 101 to 200 Bingo

Materials
- 101 to 200 Bingo Board
- One deck of Numeral Cards
- One deck of Tens Cards
- Colored pencil, crayon, or marker

Players: 2 or 3

How to Play

1. Each player takes a 1 from the Numeral Card deck and keeps this card throughout the game.

2. Shuffle the two decks of cards. Place each deck face down on the table.

3. Players use just one Bingo Board. You will take turns and work together to get a Bingo.

4. To determine a play, draw two Numeral Cards and one Tens Card. Arrange the 1 and the two other numerals to make a number between 100 and 199. Then add or subtract the number on your Tens Card. Circle the resulting number on the 101 to 200 Bingo Board.

5. Wild Cards in the Numeral Card deck can be used for any numeral from 0 through 9. Wild Cards in the Tens Card deck can be used as + or − any multiple of 10 from 10 through 70.

6. Some combinations cannot land on the 101 to 200 Bingo Board at all. Make up your own rules about what to do when this happens. (For example, a player could take another turn, or the Tens Card could be *either* added or subtracted in this instance.)

7. The goal is for the players together to circle five adjacent numbers in a row, in a column, or on a diagonal. Five circled numbers is a Bingo.

101	102	103	104	105	106	107	108	109	110
111	112	113	114	115	116	117	118	119	120
121	122	123	124	125	126	127	128	129	130
131	132	133	134	135	136	137	138	139	140
141	142	143	144	145	146	147	148	149	150
151	152	153	154	155	156	157	158	159	160
161	162	163	164	165	166	167	168	169	170
171	172	173	174	175	176	177	178	179	180
181	182	183	184	185	186	187	188	189	190
191	192	193	194	195	196	197	198	199	200

Practice Page
Different Shapes, Equal Pieces

0	0	1	1
0	0	1	1
2	2	3	3
2	2	3	3

Practice Page
Different Shapes, Equal Pieces

4	4	5	5
4	4	5	5
<u>6</u>	<u>6</u>	7	7
<u>6</u>	<u>6</u>	7	7

Practice Page
Different Shapes, Equal Pieces

8	8	9	9
8	8	9	9
WILD CARD	WILD CARD		
WILD CARD	WILD CARD		

+10	**+10**	**+10**	**+10**
+20	**+20**	**+20**	**+20**
+30	**+30**	**+30**	**+40**
+40	**+50**	**+50**	**+60**
+70	**WILD CARD**	**WILD CARD**	**WILD CARD**

Practice Page
Different Shapes, Equal Pieces

-10	**-10**	**-10**	**-10**
-20	**-20**	**-20**	**-20**
-30	**-30**	**-30**	**-40**
-40	**-50**	**-50**	**-60**
-70	**WILD CARD**	**WILD CARD**	**WILD CARD**

Practice Page A

Find the total amount of money in two different ways.

6 quarters
6 nickels
6 pennies
6 dimes

Here is the first way I found the total amount of money:

Here is the second way I found the total amount of money:

Different Shapes, Equal Pieces

Practice Page B

Find the total amount of money in two different ways.

   3 quarters
   9 pennies
   5 nickels
   4 dimes

Here is the first way I found the total amount of money:

Here is the second way I found the total amount of money:

Practice Page C

Find the total amount of money in two different ways.

     3 half dollars
     3 pennies
     7 nickels
     5 dimes

Here is the first way I found the total amount of money:

Here is the second way I found the total amount of money:

Practice Page D

For each problem, show how you found your solution.

1. There are 18 family members going on a picnic at the park in various cars. Each car holds 5 people. How may cars will be needed?

2. Five family members are making sandwiches for the picnic. How many should each one make to feed the 18 who are going?

3. The 18 family members who are going to the picnic want to drink lemonade. The group takes along five pitchers of lemonade. How many people should each pitcher be able to serve?

Practice Page E

For each problem, show how you found your solution.

1. The office in my school has a phone directory sheet with 3 columns of 46 names in each column. How many names are there on that sheet?

2. There were 46 children in each of three areas in Sol's camp this summer. How many children were at the camp?

3. Molly is planning an activity. She asked me to arrange 3 piles of toothpicks, with 46 in each pile. How many toothpicks will I need?

Practice Page F

For each problem, show how you found your solution.

1. My teacher recycles her newspapers. She can fit 5 days of newspapers into one bag. How many bags will she need for 31 days?

2. How many bags will my teacher need to recycle her newspapers of 40 days?

3. How many bags will my teacher need to recycle her newspapers of 71 days?